Land Grabbing

Land Grabbing

Journeys in the New Colonialism

BY

STEFANO LIBERTI

Translated by Enda Flannelly

VERSO

London • New York

First published in English by Verso 2013
Translation © Enda Flannelly 2013
First published as *Land grabbing. Come il mercato*
delle terre crea il nuovo colonialismo
© Minimum Fax 2011

1 3 5 7 9 10 8 6 4 2

Verso
UK: 6 Meard Street, London W1F 0EG
US: 20 Jay Street, Suite 1010, Brooklyn, NY 11201
www.versobooks.com

Verso is the imprint of New Left Books

ISBN-13: 978-1-78168-117-6

British Library Cataloguing in Publication Data
A catalogue record for this book is available from the British Library

Library of Congress Cataloging-in-Publication Data
Liberti, Stefano.
[Land grabbing. English]
Land grabbing : journeys in the new colonialism / Stefano Liberti
translated by Enda Flannelly.
pages cm
"First published as Land grabbing. Come il mercato delle terre
crea il nuovo colonialismo, © Minimum Fax, 2011."
Includes index.
ISBN 978-1-78168-117-6 (hardback)
1. Land tenure–History–21st century. 2. Land use, Rural–History–21st century.
3. Food supply–History–21st century. 4. Agriculture–Economic aspects–
History–21st century. I. Title.
HD1251.L48713 2013
333.3'1–dc23
2013018399

Typeset in Sabon by Hewer Text UK Ltd, Edinburgh
Printed in the US by Maple Press

I'm an optimist: one day the Earth
will be used to fertilise a faraway planet.

Altan

Contents

Acknowledgements

Every book is a journey, in both a physical and an internal sense. This one in particular had a long gestation period, and encompasses a quest that for one reason or another took me three years and across four continents. As I wandered I had the benefit of the help, friendship and advice of many people, who I would like to thank here in random order: Emilio Manfredi, Gianluca Baccanico, Emiliano Bos, Abdullah Abalkhail, Sami Bukhmseen, Alfredo Bini, Verena Glass, Serena Romagnoli, Cristiano Navarro from the CIMI in Dourados, Christian Brueser, Alain Gresh, Antonio Onorati, Caterina Amicucci and Luca Manes from the Campagna per la Riforma della Banca Mondiale, Joe Jordan from Soyatech, Ruxandra Lazarescu, Devlin Kuyek from Grain, Marco Bassi, Dulcineia Pavan from Sem Terra, my colleagues at *Il manifesto* with whom I learnt my trade, Silvestro Montanaro, Nino Fezza and the entire group from *C'era una volta*.

A special thanks also to the staff at Minimum Fax, who believed in this project and supported it. I am particularly grateful to Christian Raimo, who convinced me to get the book down on paper when all I could see ahead was a titanic task, and who followed me every step of the way.

Last but not least, my thanks to Giulia and Tiago, simply because they exist.

Preface to the English-Language Edition

Two years have passed since the first edition of this book. Today, land grabbing is much in the news. Newspaper reports, university conventions, and NGO launch appeals and petitions take it as their subject. But the underlying fact hasn't changed: today the race is heating up for the acquisition of arable land in the southern hemisphere – it is at its most aggressive in sub-Saharan Africa – and the stakes are higher than ever. The competitors are foreign groups intent on producing food crops or alternative fuels for other continents. Whether it is Saudi Arabian companies investing in Ethiopia to produce rice, European investment funds involved in biofuel production in Senegal or Brazilian groups obtaining hundreds of thousands of hectares in Mozambique to grow soya destined for Asia, the phenomenon continues unabated. According to estimates by the NGO Grain, which tries to keep track of these agreements, every year since 2007 has seen 10 million hectares of arable land pass from public to private hands.

Land grabbing is the new venture for entrepreneurs and businessmen, for states anxious to guarantee food for their citizens and for investors who want to multiply their profits. This rush for land is a direct consequence of the food crisis of 2007–8, when the prices of essential foods – such as rice, grain and corn – went through the roof. The increase was mainly due to the financial shock that had previously engulfed Wall Street and dragged half of the world's stock markets into a whirlpool. Reeling from the collapse of the shares market, many investors fell upon 'refuge goods' such as basic food products and land. Food and its production suddenly became the business of the future. It was a turn of events that put in question a development model – that of increasing productivity at all costs – which is also a cultural model. Apart from financial speculation, the desire to make a fast buck and the bad faith of a number of corrupt governments who undersell their nations' resources, an underlying issue has been revealed whose influence on our future is increasingly unavoidable: the rise in the world's population and the consequent decrease in the amount of food available to all.

It is with these facts in mind that I have sought to analyse the problem, by questioning the various protagonists and coming to grips with their varied points of view, in order to accurately depict a phenomenon that was largely overlooked when I first started writing this book.

Some things have changed since 2011. A number of the projects whose inception I witnessed have either failed or been suspended, like the Jatropha cultivation by a British company in Tanzania that I cover in the last chapter. Others have grown beyond measure; new groups have thrown themselves into the purchase of land and new countries – like the latest piece on the international chessboard, South Sudan – have put hundreds of thousands of hectares on the market. From an investment point of view, the trend has remained the same. Not least because global economic conditions have not changed to any great extent: the crisis in the traditional shares sector still cuts deep, and financial groups continue to place their bets on the refuge goods of land and food production.

What has changed the most, now that the spotlight is being shone on these activities, is the way they are perceived by the main parties involved: the investors, the farming organisations, the governments. Investors are wary: they know they are under fire from the international NGOs, targeted by activists and monitored by the international press. In London in December 2012, at the most recent Global AgInvesting convention for investors interested in agriculture, the communications director refused me the media pass he had given me two years previously, when I attended the same conference in Geneva, in November 2010 (see Chapter 3). He explained that it had been decided 'only uncritical journalists' were to be admitted. I was told, 'You are our adversary because your work jeopardises our business.'

For their part, small farm organisations have formed consortiums and have grown in strength. They've also made sure their voices are being heard. During an FAO regional meeting in Brazzaville, the capital of the Republic of the Congo, I witnessed how the many African organisations were now conversing with the governments as equals. The impression I had got of watching the deaf speak to one another at the FAO meeting in October 2010 had now faded. Following three years of negotiations – meaningful interaction between grass-roots organisations, governments and FAO officials – the Committee for Food Sovereignty approved a set of guidelines for access to land which, at least on paper, represent a point of reference for avoiding the more predatory forms of expropriation. The guidelines assert that states should promote a series of investment models that don't result in the large-scale transfer of land laws to investors but rather encourage partnerships with small local landholders.

Of course, these guidelines are not binding. But certainly that aura of inexorability and the advance of a seemingly unstoppable trend are now coming up against some obstacles and resistance is growing. The Tanzanian government, which initially relinquished land with considerable enthusiasm, found itself burned by a number of fraudulent deals, and has now established a strict code – at least on paper – for international investors. Other states are also questioning their approach. From this point of view, the guidelines approved at FAO represent a reference framework. 'It's up to us in civil society to ensure that they aren't merely a dead letter but that governments incorporate them into their national legislations,' I was told in Brazzaville by Mamadou Chissoko, the volcanic honourary president of Roppa, the network of small West-African peasant organisations. 'Otherwise it's like cycling on water. We don't get anywhere.' The result of dialogue between governments, civil societies and investors – a fragmentary dialogue, often steeped in incomprehension and reciprocal mistrust – will be crucial to an understanding of how the agricultural and social balances in the southern hemisphere will be structured. It will reveal whether, amid all these colossal shifts of land, some are destined to cycle on water while others continue to amass wealth with impunity. Or whether it is possible, within the limits of interests that do not always coincide, to imagine that those involved in this land rush – investors, governments, grass-roots associations and international organisations – can adopt a common path which will lead to the more sensible regulation of a worrying phenomenon that threatens to transform the borders of our planet until they are unrecognisable.

Introduction

A few weeks ago I was sitting at a table at a seaside bar-restaurant in Zanzibar, the semiautonomous island off the coast of Tanzania. I was drinking a Sprite and writing on my computer when I happened to look down at a local newspaper. FAO were ringing alarm bells over the latest increase in food prices. 'If this continues, 925 million people risk starvation.' As I was reading the article, four white men in their forties came up to the bar. They were dressed in swimming trunks and looked cold. 'If this Tanzania grain thing works out we're home and dry,' said one. 'Depends how much it's going to cost us to rent the land,' said another. 'Don't have to worry about that, our agents *in situ* say it's going to be a steal,' replied the first. Then the four of them made their way back to the beach.

What they were discussing is the subject of the book you're presently holding: the great race for land that has been going on over the past three years in a sizeable chunk of the southern hemisphere. Millions of hectares rented out to foreign businessmen, multinationals and investment funds to produce food or agrofuels destined for the northern hemisphere. Land grabbing is the new conquest area for adventurers and businessmen, for states anxious to guarantee food provision for their citizens, and for investors who want to multiply their profits.

This rush for land is a direct consequence of the food crisis that broke out in 2007–8, when the prices of essential foods – such as rice, grain and corn – went through the roof. The increase was mainly due to the financial shock that had previously engulfed Wall Street and dragged half of the world's stock markets into a whirlpool. Reeling from the collapse of the shares market, many investors fell upon 'refuge goods' such as basic food products, thus driving up prices and causing the outbreak of revolts across half the planet, from Egypt to Haiti and from the Ivory Coast to Indonesia. Today we are faced with a similar situation: the prices of basic food products are rising again, along with the price of a barrel of oil. The first uprisings are afoot. The reasons for the revolts in North Africa – especially those in Tunisia and Egypt – included the increase in the price of food. During the first insurrections in Tunisia, protesters brandished baguettes. It is more than likely that the 'perfect storm' is set to strike once more.

If many southern hemisphere countries seem once again destined to be overwhelmed, as FAO's alarm bells are indicating, others seem to have prepared themselves: states rich in liquid assets but food poor – such as the Arab Gulf States – want to avoid finding themselves in the same situation that befell them in 2008, when they were trapped by exportation bans in those countries from which they imported food. So they launched a vast campaign of land acquisition abroad, land which would be under their direct control. They produce elsewhere what they need at home. At the same time, various types of financial companies have thrown themselves onto this new golden-egg-laying goose. If food is the good to bet on, you must control its means of production, and that means controlling land. The perfect storm will do damage in many places, will have no effect in others, while in others still it will lead to considerable joy.

This book seeks to piece together this entire chain, to discover who is acquiring this land in many parts of the world, and to understand the reasons, the ambitions and the calculations that lie behind the transfer of millions of hectares. It directly questions those governments that rent out sections of their land; it gives voice to the small farmers who are fighting expropriation; and it engages with the investors who are acquiring the land. It moves between the muffled rooms of FAO and the shacks of the local people left homeless deep in the Brazilian hinterland; from the arid countryside of Saudi Arabia to the extended cornfields marked for ethanol production in the American Midwest; from the luxurious Ethiopian plateaus to the trading rooms of the Chicago stock exchange. It doesn't claim to be complete, as its subject matter is a global phenomenon involving dozens of countries. What it does do is offer several interpretations based on data that has been collected on the ground. Starting from the meetings, the interviews, the rapport established with the hundreds of men and women who have opened up their homes, their offices, and often even their hearts to me, giving me their time and answering my pressing questions, I have tried to grasp the meaning of a phenomenon that is destined to tip the balance in a large part of the southern hemisphere. I have tried to put into context the various aspects of this global upheaval which directly affects hundreds of thousands of people and, on a broader level, everybody on the planet. I have attempted to trace the causes, to understand the guidelines, to predict its future developments, while constantly reminding myself not to ignore the many facets involved and to go beyond a simple dichotomy of evil hoarders and poor dispossessed peasants. If the most visible result is precisely this – thousands of small farmers losing their land – then land grabbing cannot be reduced to a neo-colonial divestment process initiated by certain states or private companies in their dealings with other nations of dubious governance. Such an interpretation, though partly correct, is nonetheless limited, because it ignores other key aspects of the big picture, such as the total lack of investment in agriculture in the southern hemisphere over the past twenty years or the very real need for countries with unfortunate morphologies, like those in the Persian Gulf, to obtain secure food resources. The rush for land justifiably causes anxiety and passion, given that it assails that most primary and essential of goods, namely food. It puts in question a development model – that of increasing productivity at all costs – which is also a cultural model. Apart from financial speculation, the desire to make a fast buck and the bad faith of a number of corrupt governments who undersell their nations' resources, an underlying issue is revealed whose influence on our future is increasingly unavoidable: the rise in the world's population and the consequent decrease in the amount of food available to all. It is with these several aspects in mind that I have sought to analyse the problem that gives this book its title, after a long journey which has enhanced my life professionally, but even more so on a personal level. My hope is that it may somehow enhance that of its reader also.

Stone Town, Zanzibar, March 2011

CHAPTER I

Ethiopia: An Eldorado for Investors

The first thing you notice is the vastness. Flourishing lands that extend as far as the eye can see. Green hills that roll down to the banks of a crystal water lake. Just below the plateau, the harshness upon which Addis Ababa rises softens into a landscape that looks like Paradise. The sun is shining. The air is pure. It seems a world away from the stifling atmosphere in the capital, where the exhaust fumes merge with whatever little oxygen is available at an altitude of 2,300 metres. This is Awassa, in the heart of the Ethiopian Rift Valley, 300 kilometres south of Addis Ababa. The surrounding countryside is breathtaking in its beauty. The road into town is lined with the hoardings of agricultural companies. There's a symbol, a name, sometimes a telephone number of an office far away. Nothing to be seen beyond the gates, apart from endless stretches of seemingly uncultivated land.

But behind these very same gates, at a safe distance from prying eyes, lies the final frontier of this African country's agricultural development: high-tech greenhouses in which grow legumes, fruits, vegetables, or plants cultivated for the so-called agrofuels – a development that Ethiopia has entrusted to foreign investors through a gigantic long-term rental plan that has transformed it into a destination for businessmen and adventurers from the other half of the planet.

I've come here to Awassa to visit one of these agricultural companies: Jittu International. 'The most avant-garde industrial farm in all of Africa', says its manager Gelata Bijiga, with pride and a little exaggeration, as I park my car after travelling the three kilometres of dirt road that separates the entrance gates from the greenhouses.

Gelata doesn't waste much time on pleasantries. He greets me with a handshake and takes me on a tour. His boss – the Dutch agronomist Jan Prins, who I had talked to shortly before on the phone – has instructed him to show me around, and he is more than happy to do so. We enter the first greenhouse: an expanse of red tomatoes, mature and succulent. Grouped in bunches of five, they dangle with an almost unnatural symmetry from luxurious plants. As the manager leans over the seedlings, inspecting them carefully and cupping them in his hands to determine their progress, he reels off the company's statistics: a thousand hectares of land, a thousand employees and eight greenhouses – soon to be increased to sixteen.

These eight greenhouses are just the first phase of a project that is rapidly expanding. All kinds of everything are grown here, from tomatoes to aubergines, zucchinis to peppers. The produce is perfect, showing the same standard size and brilliant colours that we expect to see in the aisles of our supermarkets. Each greenhouse presents a different kind: red peppers here, green peppers there. Long aubergines here, round ones there. Some are familiar to westerners, others are more exotic, looking like the fruit of a possible alien mutation: one side of a greenhouse contains tomatoes with yellow skin and a white interior. They look strange, but taste just as good as the more common type. Gelata moves among the plants with consummate ease. He points out the various experiments. He highlights the respective qualities of each product. He offers a wealth of detail in describing the latest techniques applied to these intensive crops. 'The hoses for the irrigation system extend between the rows. The system is regulated by a centralised information system and provides the plants with precisely the right amount of water and fertilisers', he tells me enthusiastically. The project is a roaring success. The company is making huge profits. Over the next two years, the manager assures me, production will triple at the very least. Specifically engineered to cater for the target market thousands of kilometres away, these succulent tomatoes, these red, green and yellow peppers, these aubergines as smooth as a baby's skin, aren't destined for the Ethiopians, but for the infinitely wealthier consumers in the Arab Gulf states. 'Whatever we produce here is for exportation. In twenty-four hours we can transport our produce from here to the consumer, in some restaurant in Dubai.' The goods are picked and placed in crates, put in refrigerators and taken by truck to Addis Ababa. Once there, they are loaded onto planes headed for the Middle East, the United Arab Emirates or Saudi Arabia.

Just as the produce is destined for overseas, likewise the company's investors and, to a certain extent, its infrastructure are also foreign: the seeds are imported from the Netherlands, along with the computerised irrigation system; the greenhouse structures were developed by Spanish engineers, and the fertilisers also come from Europe. The firm run by Jan Prins resembles a sort of extraterritorial enclave: the irrigation system, the hyper-technological greenhouses, even the end products – so perfect because they are the result of genetic experimentation – are in total contrast with the surrounding landscape, which consists of land tilled by oxen or by farmers with hoes whose backbreaking work is done totally by hand on small plots. In the Jittu greenhouses there are computer rooms which constantly monitor the temperature, the pH of the earth, the quality of the water absorbed. Beyond the gates, the small straw and clay *tikuls* house entire families of farmers and the few animals in their possession. The feeling is one of passing, in the space of a few kilometres, from the Middle Ages to the most advanced modernity. The operation and yield of the greenhouses are certainly impressive, but appearances can be deceptive. There is one crucial aspect without which the picture is incomplete. This company, which to the locals must seem like a UFO that has chosen to land on the fields of Awassa, avails itself of two typically local elements: the land and the workforce. Elements with two characteristics that render them unbeatable: high productivity and a very low cost.

Hundreds of men and women are picking the vegetables in the greenhouses. Hundreds more work in the packing department. They work in silence, and their movements seem mechanical: one woman puts tomatoes in groups of forty in a box, another wraps them up, then a young man carries the crate to the fridge until the next truck takes it away. The room is large and well organised. The vegetables are arranged according to type. They are put into crates which are then stacked in an orderly fashion. At regular intervals someone moves them to the fridges. The average daily wage of these people is 9 birr, or 40 euro cents.

Gelata, who has an agronomy degree from Jimma University, has been working for Jittu Horticulture for three years. His salary, which he prefers not to reveal, is obviously higher than that of his compatriots who work in the fields, but he doesn't seem too scandalised by this state of affairs: 'This is Ethiopia, we can't be offering salaries higher than what is normally earned here. In any case, we give these people training. We teach them a trade.'

The Jittu company is not a sweatshop. It is simply acting within the acceptable parameters of the market, which in these parts means labour and land at dirt cheap prices, and therefore enormous profits. Besides, the Ethiopian Investment Agency, which promotes foreign investment in the country, explicitly highlights this aspect on its website: 'Labour costs in Ethiopia are lower than the African average' (www.

ethioinvest.org). Jan Prin's company has merely seized the opportunity that the Ethiopian government has been promoting for the past five and a half years to those businessmen who have a bit of money to spend and a degree of know-how to put into play. At the end of 2007, Addis Ababa launched a plan for the long-term rental of parts of its land to investors bent on making them productive. It was met with enthusiasm by groups from across the world – mostly Saudis and Indians but also Europeans – who lost no time in acquiring lands on which they could start large-scale production. They are growing, or planning to grow, all kinds of produce: rice, tea, vegetables, cereals, cane sugar, as well as many plants used for making agrofuels, from jatropha to palm oil. So far, about a million hectares have been allocated. The plan foresees the assignment over the next few years of a total of about three million hectares – roughly the same land size as Belgium. The rental rates are extremely low, ranging from 100 to 400 birr (4 to 16 euros) per hectare for one year, depending on the quality and position of the land. In Gambella, a remote region on the border with South Sudan where most of the land has been put on the market, the rent is a mere 15 birr per hectare (60 euro cents). These favourable regulations, together with low labour costs and the many other benefits bestowed by the government, make Ethiopia one of the places in the world with the highest return on investment in agriculture. 'This is an Eldorado for an agricultural investor', says a visibly pleased Gelata, while showing me a row of identical bright green zucchinis, every one just the right size to fit into a crate that will soon be closed and sent to the Persian Gulf.

The Sheikh of Addis Ababa
The wholesale leasing of Ethiopian land (and of land in many other African countries) is the result of a typical market mechanism: the meeting of an alluring offer and a rapidly rising

demand. That demand became an urgent necessity following an event of global proportions: the food crisis of 2007–8, which led to prices rocketing for basic foods such as rice, grain, corn and sugar. Although it is true that much media attention was given to the food riots that inflamed many African, Asian and Central American states, the crisis also stirred more than a few feathers in many areas that are normally less turbulent. The Arab Gulf states started to fear that they would be left without food, despite their enormous cash resources. This is because the market works in fickle ways. The hike in prices didn't just lead to an increase in costs, but also had a more dangerous medium-term effect: in many producing nations, especially those producing rice, protectionist measures began to be implemented that sought to block exportation. This led to the first shortages in importing countries, with potentially devastating effects. Alarm bells sounded in Riyadh, but also in Dubai and Abu Dhabi, leading to a new policy that was given absolute priority by those in charge: to guarantee full control of the food supply at whatever cost, in order to be immune from the storms that shake international commerce. Given that it's a Herculean task to grow rice in the desert, the Saudi rulers and their counterparts in the Emirates opted for a faster solution: to produce the food they needed elsewhere.

That perfect elsewhere was Ethiopia. Geographically close, rich with fertile land and graced with an excellent climate which permitted exceptional returns, the African country immediately revealed itself to be the best candidate for the role of 'Granary of the Persian Gulf'. Added to this was the fact that the Ethiopian land market was ready to open up to outside investors, not least due to the savvy dealings and networking skills of a man who was to establish himself as unmistakably the best negotiator in Saudi-Ethiopian relations: the billionaire Mohammad Hussein Al Amoudi. Born of an Ethiopian mother and Yemeni father, this naturalised Saudi sheikh is one of the fifty richest men in the world, according to *Forbes* magazine. A close confidante both of King Abdullah and the high command of the Ethiopian People's Revolutionary Democratic Front (EPRDF) led by Meles Zenawi,[1] the sheikh has built a veritable empire through his consortium, Midroc, which runs industries, hotels, hospitals and shopping centres. His investments in Ethiopia, like those he has made worldwide, have expanded into every sector in which there's a profit to be made: from hydrocarbon to infrastructure and from finance to telecommunications. Given the crisis brought about by the food shortages, it was inevitable that the sheikh would pounce on the latest golden-egg-laying hen: intensive agriculture. The story goes that Al Amoudi responded to the concerns expressed by the royal family in Riyadh by bringing King Abdullah a sack of rice produced in Ethiopia. The king, mesmerised by the exceptional quality of the rice, gave him carte blanche to become the overseer of the Saudi's agricultural investment plan in Ethiopia.

Whether or not there's any truth to this story, since late 2008 Al Amoudi has thrown himself into organising delegations, promoting meetings and expanding networks. This series of public relations endeavours resulted in the Saudi–East African Forum, a meeting between Saudi ministers and entrepreneurs and leaders from seven East African nations, which took place in November 2009 in Addis Ababa. The event saw the participation of representatives from fifty large Saudi companies and four of the kingdom's ministers, all with the intention of 'promoting a unique partnership between the vast technological and financial resources of the world's largest exporter of oil and the unlimited human and natural resources of the "tigers" of East Africa'.[2] Shortly before the Forum took place, Al Amoudi had created a new company – the Saudi Star Agricultural Development plc. – whose *business target* was the acquisition of land with the purpose of investing in the agricultural sector. 'Sheikh Mohammad is increasingly interested in abandoning urban areas in order to concentrate on agriculture and agricultural production', reiterated his consultant, spokesman and Saudi Star factotum, on the eve of the summit in Addis Ababa.[3]

No sooner was it said than done: from that point on, investment in the agricultural sector took off at lightning pace. Today, Al Amoudi directly controls three farms in Ethiopia, including 10,000 hectares of land in the Gambella region, where he produces rice for export to Saudi Arabia. Negotiations are underway with the government for another 300,000 hectares. Even Jittu Horticulture in Awassa is a sister company of Al Amoudi's empire. Although formally independent, the fact is that Jittu obtained the land through a concession from the sheikh, who in turn rented it from the government.

The land belongs to the people (and to those who govern the people)

In Ethiopia, the only legitimate owner of land is the state. Upon coming to power in 1991 after ousting the 'red dictator' Mengistu Haile Mariam, the EPRDF decided to maintain the same system for controlling the land that existed under the DERG socialist regime. Ethiopia at the time was a disaster zone, ravished by drought and famine, a name that conjured images of stunted children with swollen bellies, the desperate recipients of money raised by Bob Geldof, Bono and a cast of other stars at Live Aid in 1985. Many people, at the height of the collective emotion generated by this global event – the 'concert for Ethiopia' – blamed the famine on baneful land management by DERG, whose 'agrarian socialism' banned private property and tried to group or force farmers together in cooperatives under the party's control. When the rebels, led by Meles Zenawi, came to power, everybody expected them to quickly enact agrarian reform. But to the great discomfort of the international donors – primarily the World Bank and the International Monetary Fund, who were hoping for large-scale privatisation of the land – the new government immediately confirmed DERG's land policy, and then, in 1995, wrote the principle of 'the public property of land' into the constitution, with article 40 declaring that 'the land is the common property of the nations, nationality and people of Ethiopia'.[4]

According to this principle, therefore, it falls to the state, through its regional and local offices (the so-called *woreda* and *kebele*) to bestow cultivable land, and the benefactor holds no right of ownership, but is merely given permission to use the land. Inspired by the principle of egalitarian justice, this policy won the favour of rural populations, who still clearly remembered the great iniquity of the imperial period, when the land was controlled by a handful of landowners. But it also provided the government with a formidable source of power: in a country in which 85 percent of the population lives in the countryside and earns its living by farming, whoever controls the land controls the people. It is, then, the state who grants the arable land, whether to the farmers who need it for their own sustenance or to large investors, be they local or international.

But in what way and to whom is access given to what looks to be an extremely profitable investment? To find out, I pay a visit to a new residential area on the outskirts of the capital, to which a number of public offices have been moved. The area is a mass of building sites, a sign of the gigantic property boom that is changing the urban landscape here. Over the past few years, Addis Ababa has become one long and uninterrupted 'work in progress'. In every corner of the city, buildings are going up, foundations are being dug, cement is being laid, although it's difficult amid this construction fever to see any overall logic in what's being done. The Ministry for Agriculture and Rural Development is a nondescript building on one side of a pot-holed road without asphalt, further proof of the lack of planning involved in the city's development. I have an appointment here with Esayas Kebede, the Director of the Ministry's Agency for Investment, founded in 2009 to further strengthen ties between the government and potential investors. Kebede is *the* person to talk to. He is the one the investors come to see when they want to acquire land in Ethiopia, and it is on his desk that the various business plans of groups who want to enter this sector inevitably end up. It is he – at least formally – who decides if the plans are valid and if the companies are deserving of obtaining plots of land. As I look for him I wander at random through the various rooms of the Ministry. With no usher to direct me, I get a chance to observe how the different levels of power operate in an Ethiopian public office. The rooms are large open spaces: there are about ten desks on each side and an empty space in the centre. The desks are all the same size, but what differs is how full each one is: some, in fact, are completely bare. The people sitting at them have been graced with nothing more than a sheet of paper and a pen, a clear sign that they belong on the lowest rung in the ministerial hierarchy. Others are covered with file boxes, indicating that those working at them are mid-level functionaries whose job is to examine the dossiers. Then come the few who have that real and unmistakeable symbol of power: a computer.

After rambling around for about ten minutes among drowsy functionaries showing no great desire to give directions in English, I finally manage to locate Esayas Kebede. He is sat behind his desk gazing into the distance, appearing to float in a blue jacket which is at least one size bigger than it should be. The computer taking pride of place on the desk reassures me that this is a *big man*. I have contacted the right person. As I approach, he comes to meet me and shakes my hand without making eye contact. Then he asks me to follow him into a small room adjacent to his office. It's a sort of space within a space, with a wooden dividing wall that offers a degree of privacy. The room is almost bare, its only furnishings a pair of faded leather sofas and some maps on the wall, which presumably show the areas in which the government is prepared to lease land. Kebede is reserved and wary. He's met with many journalists in recent months, all of them no doubt having entered his office with the same question hovering on their lips: 'How come Ethiopia, a country that depends on international aid to feed its people, is renting land for practically nothing to foreign investors who do not produce for the local market?' So he tries to defuse the bomb even before the detonator has been activated. No sooner have we got past the formalities than he begins a long speech, with the objective of illustrating the main tenets of the policy of renting land 'aimed at modernising an agricultural sector which is too antiquated'. He points out that of the seventy-four million hectares of cultivable land in Ethiopia, only 4 percent has been handed over to the investors. And, he argues, while Ethiopia has the land and the workforce, it does not have the capital necessary to render them productive.

Kebede's style is that of a functionary mechanically reciting a story that has been specifically prepared – one he has repeated so often that eventually he almost comes to believe it. Watching him as he talks without making any gestures or showing the least bit of enthusiasm, in his oversized jacket and his platform shoes, I get the impression that he oscillates between two or three pre-prepared speeches, depending on who he is talking to. When talking to investors, he probably takes the line 'you can get rich without spending very much'. With the international donors, it might be 'we are opening ourselves up to the global market'. With the journalists the speech is more defensive, even if the leitmotif is still the same, namely 'we are doing this for the good of our country'. But here his arguments are weaker. He maintains that the leasing policy has as its objective the modernisation of agriculture, and yet he fails to offer a convincing explanation of the effects on the local population of foreign investment for the purposes of benefiting foreign markets. Instead, he limits himself to referring to the creation of jobs and the fact that, in any case, 'those lands were vacant, in disuse, underdeveloped'.

Kebede's tone is subdued, almost monotonous, even when coming out with magniloquent phrases like this one: 'What we have set out on is a great adventure which will lead to the modernisation of the agricultural sector.' And yet, as the minutes tick by, he starts to let down his guard, gradually revealing what seems to be the principal reason for the leasing plan. 'What is your financial gain from this in the short term?' I ask him insistently. As he repeats the same old tune about opening up to the market, he suddenly adds a new detail: 'And also, we urgently need money in a strong currency.' There lies the rub: the chronic need for hard currency. The country wants to modernise with dollars (or petrodollars), and in order to obtain foreign currency it is prepared to undersell its own resources. In Ethiopia the dollar is king, to such an extent that for a foreigner it's practically impossible to buy many goods, such as a plane ticket, with the local currency. Even at the airport, the entrance visa to the country costs either 20 dollars or 17 euros. 'You can't pay in birr', the immigration official had told me when I tried to give him a handful of brown notes.

The plan to rent out the land follows the same pattern: attract currency or, better still, find a way to borrow dollars that can then be reinvested. While explaining the complicated mechanisms of the letters of credit and exchange relationships set up between the Ethiopian banks and those from investing countries when a contract is signed, Kebede intimates that the main objective of the great rental plan is to fill the state coffers with foreign money which can be reinvested. He lets it be known, without ever saying it openly, that one of the key motivations for opening up to investors is to penetrate the international banking market, even at the cost of doing so in conditions of great weakness and to very little economic advantage.

When I point out to him that the rental charges are minimal with respect to market prices, he answers that rental income is not the priority. The government is mainly interested in integrating the country into the global market, he says, and therefore its main objective is to attract investment. But apart from these emphatic affirmations on the unstoppable nature of globalisation and the (modest) spin-offs at local level in terms of jobs and the creation of know-how, he still fails to explain to me the real benefits of such a large-scale investment plan.

Secret agreements and private negotiations

The great leap forward in agriculture espoused by Kebede was decided behind closed doors by government functionaries who now run the country as if it were a private practice. There were no public discussions. The leasing plan was simply announced, more to inform investors than the population, who had absolutely no say in the matter. Over the past few years, Meles Zenawi's party, the EPRDF, has gradually managed to occupy all positions of power, relegating every dissonant voice to silence or irrelevance. The May 2010 electoral campaign underway in the country at the time of my visit offers a clear example: as the country is preparing to go to the polls, Zenawi, having repeatedly announced his retirement from politics, finally bows to reason and swallows the bitter pill of offering himself as candidate for a fifth successive term in power. Addis Ababa is awash with billboards, gigantic posters, T-shirts, all sporting the premier's face. The bee, EPRDF's symbol, is everywhere, on walls, on taxi doors, even on the enormous clock in the middle of Meskel Square. The very rare posters for Medrek, the coalition of opposition parties, seem like incongruous drops in an ocean of industrious bees. The impression is that of witnessing a one-party election.

And that, effectively, is what it turned out to be. The 2010 election was merely a new chapter in the cementing of an unchallengeable power system by the EPRDF. Zenawi's government was the result of a combination of cunning, violence and opportunism, of an ability to make the most of divisions elsewhere and to use its position on the international chessboard to strengthen its control. The EPRDF has run the country since 1991 despite being dominated by the Tigrinyas, who in the ethnic composition of the Ethiopian Federation comprise about 6 percent of the population. In the 2005 election, when the party decided to carry out voting according to democratic regulations, it realised that its approval rating was considerably lower than it had expected. When the opposition won by a landslide, the Ethiopian people took to the streets to defend the electoral result that the EPRDF refused to acknowledge. To block the protests, the government ordered the security forces to shoot at the protesters. The toll was extremely heavy: at least 200 dead and 30,000 arrested. From then on, Zenawi decided that it was better not to risk his position, and did everything he could think of to guarantee absolute power for himself and his party. He silenced all criticism through a series of measures that drove the main opposition leaders into exile or jail. He closed down all press organisations that were not in line with the party. He put a muzzle on non-governmental organisations with an *ad hoc* law banning foreign NGOs and those that receive at least 10 percent of their financing from abroad (practically all of them) from getting involved in 'human and civil rights, the rights of women, of minors and the disabled, ethnic problems or conflict resolution'. He annihilated dissent and burned civil society to the ground, establishing an all-pervasive totalitarian regime in which, as a Human Rights Watch report highlighted, 'it is difficult to distinguish between state and party, and vice versa'.[5]

The results of this slash and burn policy are right there in front of me: the only remaining representatives of the opposition that mobilised thousands of people on the streets of Addis Ababa in 2005 are a few elderly citizens who run the campaign in their free time and out of their own pocket. The most authoritative of these is undoubtedly Bulcha Demeksa, an old ex-banker and ex-official of the United Nations, who is also President of the Oromo Federal Democratic Movement (OFDM), one of the parties that constitute Medrek. I go along to meet him on a pre-election afternoon at his movement's headquarters, a crumbling little villa at the end of a dirt road. He meets me in a bare and Spartan room that contains the sum total of one wooden table and three chairs. We are at the height of an electoral campaign, and yet the party headquarters is empty. No movement, no officials at work, no militants coordinating the last pre-election push. Not even a porter at the door to welcome visitors. Just one tiny poster on the entrance gate to indicate that we are at the general headquarters of one of the main opposition parties. 'When I worked for the United Nations in Nigeria, I had an office that was a hundred square metres and three secretaries, all in a beautiful building. Look where we are today, exiles in our own home, we don't even have electricity', he says with a smile.

The man is immaculately dressed, in a grey suit with a red tie, in contrast to the less elegant Ethiopian norm. His wrinkled face exudes experience; his look is passionate but steady, the look of a man who has no time for idleness and is no longer harbouring any illusions. Demeksa knows that he is a survivor; he's one of the few members of the opposition who is still free to move around. His advanced age has given him some immunity, or perhaps the air of an 'innocuous enemy' for the bosses of the ruling party. While we're talking about the election campaign, I point out the stark contrast in numbers between his supporters, totally invisible on the streets, and those of the EPRDF, who seem to be everywhere. 'The amount the government has given each candidate for electoral expenses', he says, 'is 258 birr, or just over 10 euros. EPRDF, on the other hand, uses public money to finance their electoral campaign. Given the difference in the means at our disposal, there's not much we can do.' Only a few hours earlier I had seen firsthand the ruling party's enormous mobilisation power when I attended the final rally at the civic stadium, thronged with tens of thousands of militants brought in especially for the occasion via a fleet of coaches from various parts of the country.

Under these circumstances, the opposition almost seems like a parody of itself, whose presence only serves to lend legitimacy to the democratic pretence of the party in government. I ask Demeksa why his party insists on participating in the elections despite the extraordinarily prohibitive conditions. In response, the former banker voices his opposition to the 'progressive democracy' theory. 'Today we live in an authoritarian state. The election is a joke: it's rigged, and the party in government will clean up. We will appeal. Our appeal will be denied. But at least the youngest ones among us will see that despite the repression, despite the prison terms that most of our members have been given, we have not ceased to believe in the rule of law. It certainly won't happen tomorrow, but we have faith that one day Ethiopia will be a true democracy. We have to believe this for our children.'

Demeksa's predictions duly came to pass, at least with respect to the election: the EPRDF got 99.6 percent of the votes and the opposition was left with a single seat out of 547.

Their appeal in a court of law ended in inevitable failure. As for the second part of his prediction, only time will tell.

The days and weeks following this extraordinary election result showed the true force of the international network built up over the years by EPRDF. Despite clear violations and scandalous vote rigging, especially in rural areas, not one of Ethiopia's partners dared say a word. Outraged denouncements from many human rights organisations were met with a deafening silence. Even the somewhat critical report by the European electoral observers, which indicated 'an unbalanced playing field during the electoral campaign', has been buried by later statements from the European Union's High Representative for Foreign Affairs, Catherine Ashton, who defined the vote as 'an important moment for the democratic process' and congratulated the electorate on their 'peaceful completion of the voting process and the high turnout'. If everybody rushed in to discreetly validate this farcical election, they did so because Zenawi was basically untouchable. Ethiopia is too important for the stability of the Horn of Africa, threatened as it is by the uncontrollable Eritrean regime and a perennially war-torn Somalia. The leader of the EPRDF, in western eyes, was the only one capable of maintaining unity in this heterogeneous federation which, with its eighty-four million inhabitants, is the second most populous nation in Africa. Since 2005, when the Ethiopian government initiated its policy of scrupulously repressing dissenters, international donors have not said a word. In fact, in 2008 alone they poured three billion dollars in 'humanitarian aid' into the treasury of the Ethiopian state – the highest figure for any country in sub-Saharan Africa.[6] This silence on the part of Ethiopia's national partners has become unbelievably hypocritical, given cases such as that of the thirty-six-year-old lawyer, Birtukan Mideksa, mother of a five-year-old girl and leader of one of the opposition parties, who was initially imprisoned in 2005 and then sentenced to life imprisonment in 2008 for 'high treason', simply for speaking out against electoral rigging.[7]

Despite the crackdown on the opposition, and on civil society in general, the United States and the European Union have continued to court Ethiopia, providing aid and pointing to Meles Zenawi as an example of a modern, refined politician. To give just one example: at the time of the 2005 election the then British prime minister, Tony Blair, co-opted the Ethiopian Premier in the British initiative 'Commission for Africa', a groupthink originally inspired by Live Aid, which put pressure on international donors to maintain their promises with respect to humanitarian aid, considered to be fundamental for development and economic growth.[8] The commission's final report – significantly titled *Our Common Interest* – was even co-written by Zenawi, a man considered the most significant representative of the 'new generation of modern post-cold war African leaders', as defined by former US President Bill Clinton. Over the years, the Addis Ababa strongman has been extremely adept at performing this double role: on the one hand, a veritable Dr Jekyll involved in the fight against poverty and climate change (and invited in this capacity to all the international summits), and on the other a Mr Hyde who represses all opposition, silences every dissenting voice, and imprisons or exiles anyone who does not see things his way. One group that knows only too well the force of his wrath are the journalists from *Addis Neger*, a combative independent newspaper whose entire staff was forced to flee abroad under threat of a spurious 'accusation of terrorism', and who now wander like a diaspora through other African states and the United States.[9] Likewise Berhanu Nega, who was elected mayor of Addis Ababa in 2005, imprisoned following the protests in October that same year, and forced to emigrate to Pennsylvania after spending twenty months in jail on a charge of 'genocide and treason'.

By banking on his irreplaceability and a meticulously maintained policy of alliances designed to bolster his image as 'our man in the Horn of Africa', Zenawi has built an almost rock-solid power system which now enjoys the mantle of considerable respectability, despite his authoritarian approach and clear human rights violations. If anything, his position has been cemented even further in recent years as a result of another new factor: like many of its African cohorts, the Ethiopian regime has opened up to China, throwing open its doors to companies from Beijing, which have landed in droves to build streets, dams and all kinds of other infrastructure. This new development allows Zenawi to operate on many fronts and gives him greater leeway and bargaining power when negotiating with his traditional partners. The war for influence (and market control) between China and the western powers that is being fought throughout the continent, especially in those countries that produce raw materials, unquestionably strengthens the hand of many African governments. Where previously they might have been susceptible to blackmail or pressure from their single interlocutors, they now have an extra ace up the sleeve: 'We won't accept criticism from anybody. If the western donors ever decide to leave, we will thank them for what they have done up to that point. But we will not be told what to do by alleged friends' – such were Zenawi's uncompromising words in a post-election news conference.[10]

In the view of many in opposition, the Ethiopian government's underselling of the land is all part of the same grand plan: to foster greater international support in order to stay in power *ad infinitum*. Bulcha Demeksa puts it to me this way: 'The objectives of the land leasing are primarily political. The renting of land is part of an overall strategy by which the premier's aim is to say to the international community: I cannot be replaced. This is why, as if under a spell, no one has anything to say about the strangling of the opposition, the rigging of elections or the limitations placed on the freedom of expression.' Demeksa is an Oromo. He hails from one of the regions that have been worst affected by the leasing of agricultural land. The region is an attractive proposition for investors, given that it has good links to the capital and extremely fertile land. So, obviously, the subject is close to Demeksa's heart. As he begins to talk about it, the considerable aplomb he has maintained for the entire meeting is put on hold. His anger is palpable. 'They are practically giving away our land, without even consulting us. It's scandalous', he shouts.

According to him, with the new land rental agreements Ethiopia is increasingly becoming an integral part of a much larger chain, and the party in power is an intermediary without which no one can get a piece of the action. Once influential nations have made large-scale investments in Ethiopia, through secret negotiations with the government, they will do everything in their considerable power to ensure that the government with whom they have reached agreement remains in power unperturbed.

While this argument may be seen in part as an alibi for the opposition's inaction and almost total lack of influence on a population which is anything but happy with their government, there are unquestionably many truths in what the old banker is saying. The land rental agreements – together with those for the ambitious infrastructure projects – are always reached behind closed doors, without competition or any independent evaluation of the feasibility of such projects. 'It's always the government that decides who gets the building contracts. It's the government that decides which lands to rent and to whom. We often end up learning that a certain plot has been awarded to a certain foreign company through articles that come out in the international press', says Demeksa, before concluding with what can only be a rhetorical question: 'In your opinion, what criteria does the Ministry of Agriculture use exactly, when deciding who to assign the land to?'

A red line that is not to be crossed

I put this very same question directly to Esayas Kebede himself. 'We decide who to go with depending on the experience that they have had in the sector', he answers in a professional tone. 'We analyse the company's curriculum, their business plans and their potential, and the type of cultivation that they wish to undertake. Only then do we make a decision and pass the measure on to the regional offices.' He underlines that the function of his agency is merely to coordinate and interconnect. In theory, it isn't the Ministry of Agriculture that has the last word on the assignment of land. Each area is conceded in agreement with the regional governments, who only offer lands that are not in use. 'Ours is a federation. The central government's powers on questions of a local nature are limited.' What Kebede neglects to say is that all the regional governments are controlled by the EPRDF and that the local communities have little or no say in the matter. In the local elections held in April 2008, in which the opposition refused to participate, the government and their allies gained 99.99 percent of the vote and thus total control at all levels of public administration. The regional and district offices all fell into the hands of administrators intimately linked to those in power, and thus played their part in the building of a gigantic and sprawling system of control. The fact is that it is the administrators of the districts and the villages who regulate access to food aid programmes, jobs, houses, land, and even small loans. In controlling these sectors – which are key to the population's survival, especially in rural areas – these people have transformed themselves into something not dissimilar to squires. With one significant difference: given that their power is revocable, they must continually show themselves to be doing an excellent job. And so they zealously throw themselves into their roles as 'leaders', by assembling their own local surveillance network which ends at their door. In this Orwellian state of affairs, built on patronage, favours and informers, nobody dares raise a dissenting voice. All of which plays into the hands of the government, allowing it to maintain the impression of transparency by involving the regional bodies in the process of assigning land and whatever else.

This is why the underselling of land – which in other African countries has resulted in all-out revolt – is occurring here in a seemingly peaceful manner, without provoking unrest or even debate in the press. The only scenes of revolt were seen recently in the frontier region of Gambella, where unidentified armed men entered the Saudi Star compound and killed ten workers, including six Pakistani agronomists. Apart from this episode, which hasn't been fully explained and has been linked to political tension in the region, the underselling of land has generated no significant debate or any kind of resistance from public opinion. This was clearly explained to me by a representative of one of the few NGOs still operating in the country, but only after I had promised repeatedly that under no circumstances would I quote his name, and that his anonymity was totally guaranteed. As soon as we meet, outside a theatre in the centre of Addis, he proposes an 'early lunch', and although it's barely eleven o'clock and I'm not the least bit hungry, I follow him into a nearby restaurant. He chooses an inconspicuous table in a corner at the end of a deserted patio and orders two plates of fried fish and salad. Then we get to the reason why he has subjected me to this supplementary food intake in the middle of the morning. 'We'll get some peace here. Nobody will bother us.' As we talk about this and that – the political situation in Ethiopia, the election that has just taken place – the man answers my questions and studies me carefully. He's friendly enough but a little distrustful. He has a subtle quiet voice that doesn't quite fit a robust physique that's beginning to show the first signs of obesity. His sly expression intermittently lights up with sudden friendly bursts, interrupted every now and then by little chuckles that seem more like nervous tics than signs of amusement. He circles around my questions without letting down his guard. When I ask him how come he's still able to work, given that most organisations have been forced to close down, he says that he has been able to establish a 'continuous dialectic rapport with the government'. A metaphor I interpret as: 'we are constantly under surveillance'. When I ask him what he thinks of the election results, he flatly responds that the EPRDF has the country in its hands, without mentioning the accusations of vote rigging that have been made in many circles. But as soon as I mention the subject of land leasing – which wasn't the topic I had spoken to him about on the telephone – his tone suddenly changes. He starts looking worriedly around him. His eyes fall to his plate. Then he raises them. He scrutinises the few customers present in the restaurant. Finally he leans towards me, and in a barely audible voice lets me know that the subject is taboo. 'That's a very sensitive issue, we can't even mention that. It's part of the so-called "red line" that is not to be crossed.' Because the issue is so sensitive, nobody is subjecting it to scrutiny. No one in Ethiopia dares cross the so-called red line. 'No one really knows which lands or how many lands have been assigned, because there are no independent studies, nor could there be under these conditions', he whispers, implicitly telling me that he considers the situation scandalous but that if he wants to avoid his organisation being shut down within twenty-four hours he needs to steer well clear of any possible criticism.

It is for such reasons, then, that little is known of the size of the phenomenon: the only data available comes from the government, who talk of one million hectares already leased and another two million or so to be leased in the near future. But the rental agreements are not available for scrutiny. They are negotiated in secret, in a manner that Kebede describes as standard, and subject to no form of verification whatsoever. The little information that does get out comes from articles in the foreign press, from notifications by companies that have obtained the land, and from objections made by members of the Ethiopian diaspora, who themselves very often do not have the benefit of firsthand information but have to rely on the international press.

'Ethiopia does not exist'

This becomes clear to me at an academic meeting organised by the Oromo opposition that I've decided to attend, given that it is entirely dedicated to the question of land. The seminar has a telling title: 'The Scramble for Land. Investment and Environmental Degradation in Oromia. Consequences for the Future'. Needless to say, it is being held not in Ethiopia but in a university conference hall in central London.

The meeting takes place on a Saturday in July in an underground room in City University, where the ambience is like that of an informal buffet. The weather outside is beautiful and the public parks have been invaded by throngs of semi-naked youths making the most of the few days of heat afforded by the English climate. The campus, on the other hand, is deserted, as is the entire surrounding neighbourhood which feeds off the university. The only souls in view are the porters, who don't look too pleased at the weekend overtime they've been forced to do. The meeting is attended by around thirty people. The speakers all know each other: they are part of a group that meet each summer to discuss a specific topic. 'This year,' one of the organisers tells me, 'we've chosen the subject of the land because it represents the latest attack on our culture. It's colonialism in the twenty-first century, by which Zenawi's government aims at wiping out the Oromo tradition once and for all.'

The tone of the talks is hard-hitting. The definition of Ethiopia itself is questioned, given that it is, in the words of one of the speakers, 'an arbitrary creation, the result of the invasion of the southern areas by the inhabitants of the high plain'. The phenomenon of the leasing of agricultural land – referred to by the negative term *land grabbing* – is seen as merely the latest heinous act by a dictatorial government 'that doesn't acknowledge differences, one that suppresses dissent and whose policy for the past twenty years has been to deliberately wipe out local cultures from the country's social panorama'. These claims by the Oromo people – the largest ethnic group in Ethiopia – are not new. All of the speakers call into question the notion of 'ethnic federalism', the ingenious ploy by which the Tigrinyas have managed to hold onto power for twenty years, playing on a form of decentralisation that is in fact nothing other than a system of co-optation by obliging elites.[11]

The talks are all very similar to one another. The speakers, Ethiopians for the most part, have travelled from the United States and various other countries. They are anthropologists, sociologists, economists, and they all have very distinguished titles: at least in theory, they are the leading experts on the topic at hand. But the content of their talks is vague and often ideological. At times the subject is hardly touched upon: things are taken for granted, without facts and figures. Rather than an exchange of information or a brainstorming exercise on an extremely topical subject, the convention takes on the tone of a political debate between people who presently have no influence, nor are likely to in the near future, over their country's political decisions.

The reason for this somewhat superficial approach is plain: most of the speakers are exiles, people who have escaped Ethiopia in fear of persecution, and can therefore only manage sporadic contact with their native country. The information they do have is second or even third hand, not least because in Ethiopia the communications network, entirely controlled by the state telephone company, is presumed to be under constant surveillance. Even if it is not, the fear that it might be acts as an excellent deterrent. Ever since the 2005 election, when the calls to protest went out via text messages, Zenawi's government has made total control of the communications system an absolute priority. At the height of the disturbances, it simply blocked the possibility of sending text messages for two years. Then it refined its technique, procuring a Chinese software technology which allowed it to encrypt all exchanges of information, whether vocal or written. This development led *The Economist* to write, on the eve of the 2010 election, that 'while in other African nations people wonder whether it's better to have a Blackberry or an iPhone, in Ethiopia people wonder whether or not it is possible to have a phone'.[12]

The talks I listen to at City University clearly demonstrate that pervasive control of communications – together with the government's other repressive measures – have succeeded in impeding the flow of information. So, while a professor offers a long and interesting digression on how EPRDF took power and on their land policy, he refers to the present situation only *en passant* and in an almost didactic manner. An anthropologist talks about the evacuation of an indigenous community in Oromia – which happened twenty years ago. Nyikaw Ochalla, an Anauk activist – an ethnic group present in the border region of Gambella – speaks about the 'last phase of a genocide that has been going on for years'. He points out that most if not all of the agricultural areas used as pastures by the Anauks have been handed over to international investors. He tells of how the land around his village has been completely privatised and how, as a result, the villagers have all been reduced to working as day labourers. Even his speech, albeit more articulate than those that preceded it, has the ring of old news. When I ask him which companies have obtained land in Gambella, he mentions Karuturi, a large Indian group whose acquisition of 300,000 hectares has been amply covered in the international press. When I ask for clarification on the real extent of the phenomenon in his region, he is unable to provide me with precise figures. A political refugee in the United Kingdom, Ochalla is one of the world's leading experts on the Anauks, one of the indigenous groups to have suffered most from the Addis Ababa elite's policy of hoarding collective resources. As someone who has fled from persecution, he has the Anauk question in his blood. He knows only too well the story of his group, from the persecutions carried out by the Mengistu regime to the hopes initially raised by EPRDF and then betrayed by new expropriation policies that were now culminating with the selling-off of the land. Ochalla has a wealth of friends and relatives in the Gambella region, and tries to follow every new development. But even he admits to being helpless: he hasn't set foot in his region in ten years and has difficulty getting fresh information. 'Even if they know well that it's potentially devastating, people are afraid to talk about this subject', he admits in a dispirited tone. 'For this reason, it's plain sailing for the government.'

The convention ends with a press release, but it is circulated only on the sites of the Ethiopian diaspora and uses high-sounding but not particularly incisive language to denounce the land grabbing, 'proposing to coordinate a global effort to inform public opinion worldwide about this irresponsible behaviour by the multinationals'.

The Bangalore estate owners

Who are these companies that are lining up to occupy Ethiopian land? 'There are many kinds', says Kebede, 'we principally focus on the trustworthiness of the companies before assigning them land'. In reality, the lion's share – especially at this initial phase during which the lands have been assigned but the exploitation is just beginning – is taken by groups or persons who were already operating in Ethiopia and enjoyed good connections with the government. We therefore have the above-mentioned companies belonging to Sheikh Al Amoudi, or at least those who answer to him, and on whose farms the produce at present includes fruit and vegetables, but above all rice, cultivated and refined *in situ* before being exported to Saudi Arabia. The sheikh, however, has plans to expand, and has established *ad hoc* alliances with groups specialising in agribusiness: he wants to set up a 30,000 hectare sugarcane plant in the northeast in collaboration with Syngenta, and a 100,000 hectare one dedicated to biodiesel in the Benishangul Gumuz province together with the Malaysian firm Agri Nexus. These projects are still being defined, but given Al Amoudi's connections with the Ethiopian government, a positive result is practically certain.

There are many small plots that the government has ceded to its political friends abroad, from the ex-President of Nigeria, Olusegun Obasanjo, to the current President of Gibuti, Ismael Omar Guellah, who received respectively 2,000 and 4,000 hectares in Oromia.[13] But the largest agricultural investor in the country is an Indian group with its headquarters in Bangalore: the Karuturi group mentioned by the Anauk activist at the London convention. The leading producer of roses in both Kenya and Ethiopia, this company has decided in the past two years to accept the Ethiopian government's proposal to diversify its activity. It's not the only one: other, smaller producers of roses, badly burned by an economic crisis that hit secondary goods such as flowers, have converted at least a part of their cultivation to the growth of foodstuffs. Karuturi is thinking much bigger, however, acquiring 10,000 hectares 250 kilometres from Addis Ababa, and another 300,000 (a territory the size of Luxembourg) in the Gambella region. Working in this area on the border with South Sudan offers an incomparable advantage: the land is free. The Indian company has concluded a one-sided agreement with the Ethiopian government: for the first six years it won't pay any rent. After that, it will pay 15 birr (60 euro cents) per hectare for the next eighty-four years. By the company's own admission, land of the same quality in Malaysia or in Indonesia would cost about 300 euros per hectare a year.

Unlike the Saudis, who produce for export to their own country, Karuturi has a more global approach: it grows roses for Europe, and palm oil for the Indian and African markets – especially those countries in COMESA (Common Market for Eastern and Southern Africa), whose free trade agreement Ethiopia is thinking of joining to avoid paying duties on its exports.[14] Karuturi plans to grow cereals for export within Africa. The Indian company has given itself multiple objectives in order to be in a position to respond to shifts in the market. Its Managing Director, Sai Ramakrishna Karuturi, has no doubts about the policy: 'Everyone is investing in China for industry, and in India for services. For food the place to come is Africa.'[15] Esayas Kebede agrees with him, maintaining that Ethiopia is the most attractive country in the whole area. 'Everything grows in Ethiopia. All you have to do is plant. We offer conditions that very few others can offer', he adds, probably referring not only to the quality of the land and the excellent climate but also the incredibly favourable terms his agencies offer investors.

In fact, the government doesn't seem particularly interested in which products are to be grown, nor does it seem to have a genuine agricultural development strategy. It allocates the land and nothing more. 'Initially, we thought about concentrating primarily on biofuel, but for the moment this has stalled somewhat', Kebede concedes.

This comment by the Chief of the Agency for Investment is nothing if not an understatement: more than 'concentrating primarily on biofuel', Ethiopia at one stage had the grandiose if fleeting dream of becoming the Brazil of Africa, the largest producer of agrofuels in the entire continent. In September 2007, shortly before the more general land leasing policy was made official, the government published its 'Biofuel Development and Utilisation Strategy'.[16] It argued that the country was too dependent on fossil fuels, and declared itself ready to assign 23.3 million hectares to the production of biofuels. At a time during which both the United States and the European Union had a declared objective to increase the use of these kinds of fuels, the Ethiopian government caught a serious dose of the biofuel bug. But the plans it had were megalomaniac: the land mass allocated was more than a quarter of the country's total cultivable land. The great plan was for intensive monoculture, entrusted to 'local or international investors to whom land would be assigned at no cost through long term rental agreements'.

At first the offer was accepted by a handful of pioneers, a number of whom began to produce a moderate amount of palm oil, others jatropha, still others castor oil for biodiesel. But the sector never took off, and the few who had thrown themselves into the adventure got burned. A German company, Flora Eco Power, which had been given 8,000 hectares in Oromia for castor oil production, went bust after managing to export only three types of seeds to Germany, long before reaching full activity. An American company, the Ardent Energy Group, decided to return to 'the local farmers' the 15,000 hectares that they had been assigned for jatropha production. The British company Sun Biofuels, which has sizeable projects in Mozambique and Tanzania, maintains a claim in Ethiopia that it uses as a sort of laboratory, where it 'experiments with planting techniques and plant growth models'.[17] Fri-El Green Power, an Italian company which took over a state agency in the Nationalities and Peoples' Regional State (SNNPRS), the southern nations region, still hasn't begun production. Of the seventy firms that have obtained a licence to work in the clean fuel sector, only ten have actually started to operate, and many of these are still at a purely embryonic stage.[18] The point is that, in this field, Ethiopia is hampered by limitations of a morphological nature: the country doesn't have direct access to the sea and, given the conflictual relations between itself and Eritrea, it cannot use the port of Massawa. Produce must be transported to Gibuti, which entails travelling hundreds of kilometres along tortuous roads. An unavoidable drawback, this distance from the ports works in favour of other nations who are not so unfortunate, such as Tanzania or Mozambique, where the sector has actually seen double-figure growth. Despite the declarations of the government, who claimed to want to achieve 'energy independence', these products were also primarily destined for the foreign market. 'The sector has come to a standstill,' admits Kebede, before adding: 'We have not abandoned our goal of reaching energy independence. It is a necessary step towards becoming a modern country.'

From food to dams, a single model
Energy is the other big obsession of the EPRDF government. Over the past ten years, Addis Ababa has begun an enormous dam-building project to produce hydroelectric energy for both internal use and for exportation. This plan moved forward not least thanks to aid from foreign donors, including the World Bank and the European Investment Bank, together with credit

secured through the Italian Development Cooperation and very affordable loans from China, who in return secured the contracts for the construction of the infrastructure.

Characterised by work begun without environmental impact studies and without informing the local population in advance, and by negotiations carried out in secret in order to secure the necessary finance, the story of the dams is typically Ethiopian, and is linked in many ways to that of the leasing of land. Anyone who wishes to understand how the process works need look no further than the case of the Gilgel Gibe II dam, on the Omo river, which was built by the Italian firm Salini. The dam was financed by a massive 'credit aid' of 220 million euros from the Italian Cooperation, despite the disapproval of the Ministry for Finance and the Managing Director of the Cooperation for Development itself. As if by magic, immediately after the concession of the loan, Italy cancelled its bilateral progressive debt with Ethiopia – approximately 332.35 million euros. By effectively transforming a loan into a gift, it established that Italian public funds were to be used to build a dam in Ethiopia, with the work carried out by an Italian firm which had won the contract in unclear circumstances. How did all this come about? It was the result of Salini's excellent contacts within the Ministry for Foreign Affairs, which promised to release the loan in order to convince the Zenawi government that the project should be entrusted to an Italian firm without any allownce for competing bids. Following a series of ordeals, the dam was completed in January 2010, only for an internal tunnel to collapse two weeks after the inauguration thereby forcing the plant to cease all activity.[19]

Despite this, Salini was also handed the contract for another dam downriver from the first, the Gilgel Gibe III. This is to be a 240-metre high mega dam, and according to experts and activists will have devastating effects on hundreds of thousands of people in both Ethiopia and Kenya, where Lake Turkana will suffer an acute lowering of its waters.[20] In addition to the dams on the river Omo (the sites are already open for Gibe IV and Gibe V, whose feasibility studies have been entrusted to Chinese companies), other dams have been planned and inaugurated in various other parts of the country, in particular along the course of the Blue Nile and its tributaries, which has enraged the Egyptians and led to threats of retaliation for the failure to uphold agreements on the sharing of the water from Africa's longest river.

The issue of the dams is linked to that of the land for many reasons. Firstly, it concerns the intensive exploitation of the other resource that Ethiopia has in abundance, namely water. Secondly, it represents another 'red line' not to be crossed. It is practically impossible in Ethiopia to obtain information on the progress of the various works, not to mention the eventual negative consequences and the uprooting of indigenous communities caused by these projects. In the South Omo region alone, the government has suspended sixty-three local associations, revoked the licences of radio stations, and arrested for 'treason' a man who had worked as an interpreter for a foreign research mission concerned with Gibe III.[21] Thirdly, the development of these dams presents the same beneficial collateral effects that old Demeksa was talking about: giving the work to foreign companies strengthens common strategies for mutual advantage and intensifies collaboration networks which propel the nations involved into doing their utmost to keep those in power in Ethiopia right where they are.

There is, however, a fourth aspect that links the dam building to the land leasing even more closely. The dams will not only enable the production of electricity. They will also be systems capable of regulating water resources and water flow, useful for large-scale irrigation projects. What was initially suspected by only a few activists has subsequently been irrefutably confirmed by a study undertaken by the Ethiopian Ministry for Agriculture and Rural Development concerning the SNNPRS, the region where the Omo river flows. This study speaks of 180,000 hectares of agricultural land to go to investors right beside where Gibe III will be built. Land which is, according to the text, 'excellent for the cultivation of cotton, sesame, peanuts, palm oil' and which can be 'irrigated by the river Omo'.[22]

As part of the land leasing policy, the use of water for irrigation is included in the price. Water is not lacking in the country and the government in its wisdom has decided to supply it for free to investors. In many cases, however, this water is being taken from other users. The lands rented to Karuturi and Al Amoudi in the Gambella region are located on the banks of the area's main water tributaries, which are a primary source of life for the indigenous population. As Ochalla protests: 'The Saudi Star project uses the water reserves of the Aloworo river, upon which 20,000 people depend for fishing, agriculture and water consumption. This river and its environs are also inhabited by species of wild animals, fish and birds who risk extinction because of intensive agriculture.'

In Awassa, the 'most avant-garde agricultural business in all of Africa', set up by Jittu International, has come up with a more modern system. The water for the irrigation of its eight ultra-modern greenhouses is taken directly from a deep well that the firm itself has dug. Gelata Bijiga proudly shows me the whole mechanised system, which starts from a big tank and provides all that is necessary for the irrigation and the maintenance of the greenhouses.

The farm benefits from a flourishing environment: water isn't scarce and the land is fertile. But as I look around, I can't help asking myself who lived off this land before it was handed over to Jittu. I put the question to Gelata. At first he sidesteps, saying that the land was not utilised, before murmuring that, yes, at the beginning when they put up the fences, 'we had some problems with a few farmers who wanted to knock down our fences and bring their animals onto our land to graze, but then the police intervened and everything returned to normal'.

Other episodes of this kind in more remote regions are also whispered about in Addis Ababa. But verification of any kind is impossible. The red line is not to be crossed. The leased lands, according to the government's official version, are uninhabited and unutilised. And whoever dares say anything different is an enemy of progress and, as such, must be punished.

CHAPTER 2

Saudi Arabia: Sheikhs on a Land Conquest

The road is an asphalt tongue that rolls through a landscape without attractions: small cement constructions that appear incongruously amongst the sand, sporadic signposts showing directions for the holy cities of Mecca and Medina, isolated palm trees that bob in the wind like buoys in the midst of an open sea. Only the occasional camel traipsing away in the distance breaks the monotony of an ochre horizon of dust and stones. All else is just trucks slowly rattling along, a few cars loaded with men and women (the latter, as per the law, never at the wheel), and a few mumbled words with Amal, the Bengalese driver who has lived for ten years in Riyadh and sums up his days with a formula that seeps with boredom and exhaustion: 'work, sleep, sleep, work'. Then, as the region around the Saudi capital is gradually left behind and we get closer to Kharj, about a hundred kilometres further south, the setting changes: the greenery, initially only hinted at, suddenly explodes into a series of small and medium-sized agricultural plots. Here we see big greenhouses covered with white plastic sheets, which look like a cluster of igloos that have somehow been deposited in the desert. Before long we pass wooden buildings full of hens, or so we assume from the unmistakeable acrid stench of poultry breeding. The roadsides are lined with rows of date trees, not surprising considering that Saudi Arabia is one of the biggest producers in the world and that dates here enjoy a cult status, complete with specialised markets full of stalls that sell every kind and size imaginable. At these markets you are invariably welcomed with a little sheet listing the various types of dates, their origin, how mature they are and the level of sucrose they contain. If you have the effrontery to say 'Half a kilo of dates please, you choose', you are bound to be met with a look of disapproval and a further explanation of the many different varieties available, until eventually your patience runs out and you leave without buying anything.

Driving on towards Kharj, we start to see more traditional vegetable fields: zucchini, tomatoes, aubergines, broccoli. Among the furrows of the ploughed land, layers of protective plastic act as mini-greenhouses, aimed at making the most of every last drop of water even when it turns to gas, something that doesn't take too long in these parts. All of this sudden greenery is the result of a massive programme of state grants launched in the 1970s by the Saudi government with a specific objective in mind: to guarantee food security without depending too much on imports. An extremely costly production system, financed by petrodollars, is irrigated by drilling to unprecedented depths to reach a water source far underground.

This all came about following the 1973 oil crisis, when the West reacted to a crude-oil export freeze by the OPEC countries by threatening to use 'the food weapon' – a freeze on the exportation of food. The sheikhs in power in Riyadh decided to make provisions for such an eventuality. The reasoning was apparently simple: it made more sense to use the manna that was the abundance of oil to ensure food independence than to end up with the coffers full of money but a larder that was totally bare. If the OPEC countries could turn off the tap, then the West could retaliate by starving them out. And on this score, Saudi Arabia found itself in the unenviable position of being the cartel's most vulnerable country. Many different policies to stimulate food production were introduced during this period. In 1978, a support programme for grain production began. Presented by the state as 'a positive response by the private sector to public intervention',[1] it actually consisted of a massive system of subsidies by which the state bought up all that was produced at prices that were much higher than the market value: when it was launched, the programme stipulated a payment of 933 US dollars for every tonne of grain produced, when the real market price was 165 dollars.[2] Faced with such a disproportionate difference, the farmers quickly rose to the occasion: by 1984 Saudi Arabia had reached self-sufficiency in grain and by 1992 had risen to become the world's sixth-largest producer of the golden cereal.

These days the wind has changed. The Saudi managers have realised that the water at their disposal is an exhaustible source, just like the oil. Without the benefit of lakes or rivers, the kingdom was forced to keep digging deeper for water sources that were bound to run dry sooner or later. Eventually the government decided it simply wasn't worth their while, and began to gradually phase out subsidies for grain production, to the point that they will have completely ceased by 2016. In 2008, for the first time in thirty years, the kingdom imported 880,000 tonnes of wheat.

But the problem remains. In fact, it has gotten bigger: Saudi Arabia now has twenty-six million inhabitants, and according to projections this will rise to thirty-nine million by 2035. How can a country whose population is increasing exponentially, and whose morphology is so unfriendly that it is known as the 'kingdom in the desert', hope to guarantee food security for its citizens and for the millions of immigrants living within its borders? After the threats made, but never enforced, during the post-1973 period, another alarm bell sounded with the food crisis of 2007–8. While hunger riots were erupting across the southern hemisphere following increases in food prices, a silent tsunami was also making its way through the influential palaces of the Arabian peninsula. The top dogs in Saudi Arabia, but also in Qatar, Kuwait and the United Arab Emirates, were taking stock of the ban on exports and the various disincentives put in place in many countries – including India, Argentina, Ukraine and Vietnam. That year in particular, they were not able to buy enough rice to meet the internal demand. The managers in Riyadh realised that the market could let them down, despite their unlimited funds. In their compromised position – as the world's second-largest importer of rice, largest importer of barley (mostly used for animal feed), and soon-to-be large-scale importer of grain due to the abolishing of the subsidies – the Saudis felt the ground tremble beneath their feet. Since they couldn't trust the international market, nor produce the food needed internally, they knew they had to come up with a new strategy.

When it came, it was met with enthusiasm by King Abdullah: 'controlled externalisation'. Saudi investors would indeed provide what was necessary, only not on Saudi soil but abroad, by renting fertile lands as required. Although these lands were outside the kingdom, they would still be run by Saudi groups. The King Abdullah Initiative for Saudi Agriculture Investments Abroad (KAISAIA) was launched with great pomp and circumstance in January 2009, with an initial budget of three billion riyals (about 620 million euros) in order to encourage – through generous loans and other forms of easy payment – Saudi investors interested in exploring foreign markets.[3] Delegations of academics, government officials and investors visited those countries that looked most promising from the point of view of proximity and conditions on the ground. They travelled to Sudan, Ethiopia, Egypt and Turkey, but also to the Philippines, Vietnam and the Ukraine. Not long after the initiative was launched the first contracts were signed, the first projects inaugurated, the first cultivations set in place. As mentioned in the previous chapter,

Mohammed Hussein Al Amoudi's Saudi Star began producing various types of vegetables as well as rice in Ethiopia. Foras International – a group with its headquarters in Gedda that uses funds from the Islamic Development Bank, the Riyadh government and other private investors – acquired land in Senegal, Mali and Mauritania with the objective of producing rice for the Saudi market.[4] Hail Agricultural Development, which specialises in grain production, has rented tens of thousands of hectares in Sudan to produce cereal and import it back to its native land, and has plans to expand further into Turkey and Kazakhstan.[5]

The silence of the dragon

This land rush, which began around the beginning of 2008, was facilitated through a series of agreements – negotiated for the most part behind closed doors – made by governments who either invested directly or, as was more often the case, provided public relief and easy terms to private enterprises that were interested in the adventure. This movement saw a surprisingly low degree of involvement by one country that normally played a lead role in investments in the southern hemisphere – China. Traditionally very active in Africa, especially with regard to the exploitation of primary materials and the building of infrastructure, the Chinese have in this instance kept a relatively low profile. Despite many newspaper reports affirming the opposite,[6] Beijing businesses are not heavily involved in large-scale agricultural projects abroad, be it in Africa or elsewhere. There have been a number of initiatives by Chinese companies, especially in Sierra Leone, Zambia and Liberia, but nothing that suggests an overall strategy of 'controlled externalisation' like that pursued by the Saudis. The Chinese invasion is something of a stereotype that has by now become self-propagating: given the common perception, especially in the West, as soon as the hoarding of land in Africa is mentioned thoughts turn to masses of Chinese moving in to uproot African farmers and take control of their land. In fact, nothing of the kind has happened: there hasn't been significant investment, nor has there been a mass emigration of Chinese peasants to the virgin lands of the continent. The projects that companies from Beijing are involved in are relatively small, and they generally produce for the internal market. They were also launched long before the explosion of the 2007–8 food crisis, and in many cases they are the consequence of cooperation programmes begun in the 1970s that were subsequently taken over by entrepreneurs who transformed them into for-profit businesses.[7]

Even if officials in the Peoples' Republic have actually considered the outsourcing of agricultural production due to the decreasing amount of cultivable land in the country, no official policy to that effect has been set in motion. In the words of an official from the Ministry for Agriculture in Beijing, 'it isn't realistic to cultivate cereals abroad, and especially not in Africa and South America. Considering that many people are starving in Africa, it's just not possible to export produce from there to China. The costs would be extremely high, as would be the risks.'[8]

At the present time, Chinese investments in agriculture are made by medium- and small-sized private firms, and their degree of development is not particularly noteworthy. Even the leasing project that Beijing is negotiating with the Democratic Republic of Congo (DRC) to establish an extensive palm oil plant is aimed more at fuel development than food produce.[9]

Naturally, it can't be categorically affirmed that this policy will not change in the near future. China does have a very real problem, with 20 percent of the world's population but only 7 percent of its cultivable land. Its forced urbanisation policy and furious rate of development have brought the country very close to the critical threshold of 120 million hectares of cultivable land established by officials in Beijing. According to reports in the *Financial Times*, in 2008 the Ministry for Agriculture was about to approve a plan that supported the acquisition of agricultural land abroad, only to cancel it at the last minute.[10] Certain projects might suggest the possibility of a sharp rise in the externalisation of agricultural production – such as the financing of various dams in Mozambique and Ethiopia which would permit the creation of irrigation systems and an increase of agricultural production. Discussion on this is ongoing among Chinese officials, but for the moment no public policy of this kind has been adopted, no large-scale investment approved, no 'land rush' launched. One of the most in-depth studies on the question of the hoarding of land holds that 'up to this point there are no notable examples of land acquisition in Africa by the Chinese, apart from 50,000 hectares for which agreements have been concluded and projects developed'.[11]

Why is it that China, which undoubtedly has both the necessary connections with various African governments and the know-how to set up extensive production for exportation, hasn't gotten in on the act? Firstly, because it doesn't feel the same sense of urgency that is driving the Gulf states to act. While it may be near the critical threshold line, it still has vast areas of cultivable land and has thus far been able to guarantee its numerous inhabitants the food they require. Secondly, because it's much further away from the more 'desirable' countries than Saudi Arabia or Qatar.

The last but by no means least important reason is the one put forth by the official from the Ministry of Agriculture: land leasing agreements are very controversial. They cause resentment in the civil societies of the countries concerned and provoke the wrath of awareness campaigns in the northern hemisphere. And they fit in perfectly with accusations of neo-colonialism, which China already faces over its other investments in Africa. This is an aspect to which Beijing is particularly sensitive. As part of its policy to open up to the outside world it has continually sought to present itself as a model country which uses the benefits of its own experience to help its partners emerge, while being very careful not to attract the kind of antipathy to which ex-colonial powers are often subjected. The deep-rooted idea in the West that China is invading Africa is a conviction that, with a few exceptions,[12] is not widely shared in the continent in question. The leaders of the People's Republic have always strived to convey the idea that they are different from the others, that they invest for the reciprocal benefit of both sides and put to good use the experience they have built up during their remarkable growth. So far, they have largely succeeded in winning the approval not only of the governments with whom they have done business, but also of a large section of public opinion. 'If the Chinese will sell us three cars at the same cost that the Europeans will charge us for one, the direction we take is one dictated by logic. China gives us the possibility to negotiate on many fronts'[13] – such was the clear statement of the Senegalese President, Abdoulaye Wade at the African Union–European Union summit held in Lisbon in December 2007, during which Brussels was determined at all costs to seal free trade agreements with African countries that would actually offer the Africans precious few advantages. The truth is that China has built up a good name for itself in Africa because it doesn't insist on having its own way. Apart from the 'One China' clause, which rules out the diplomatic recognition of the Republic of Taiwan, it places no other conditions on the countries in which it invests. As one West African official put it to me on the fringes of that same Lisbon summit: 'The Chinese listen to us, they make proposals but they let us decide. The Europeans, on the other hand, just want to dictate.'

'A *philanthropic initiative*'

If the Chinese are lagging behind, the Arabic nations – especially those on the Persian Gulf – have gotten off to a flying start in the great rush for agricultural land. To get a realistic idea of the extent of the phenomenon and to hear firsthand the thoughts of those leading the race, I paid a visit to Riyadh in December 2010. The occasion is a unique one: The Gulf Research Center in Dubai has come to the Saudi capital to organise a very high-level conference on 'Gulf Investment in Africa'. This not only gives me a chance to meet the various people directly involved, but also allows me to obtain an entrance visa to Saudi Arabia, a country that doesn't normally welcome journalists.

With my business visa safely in hand, I land in the Saudi capital after a comfortable flight on a Saudi Arabia Airlines plane that is so empty that the air hostesses come through with the in-flight services three times out of sheer boredom. The airport is deserted and eerily silent: high ceilings, a fountain spraying water in the middle of a room, a large photo of Mecca. There isn't a soul to be seen. I follow the directions for passport control, happy in the knowledge that getting through shouldn't take too long, only to turn a corner and be met with a demoralising scene up ahead: a human wall of Indian and Pakistani immigrants trailing back in an endless queue from the desk reserved for foreigners. The queue is practically stationary, one person going through every five minutes. I start to prepare myself mentally for a night at passport control, cursing the fact that my plane had landed ten minutes late now leaving me at the end of this line, even though I really had no idea how long the people in front of me had been waiting. Just as I'm starting to look for some corner in which to lie down, I'm approached by an official with a long beard and rather wild eyes. 'Are you from India?' he asks me. 'I am not', I answer. 'Please, come this way', and he leads me to an empty aisle where my passport is taken and promptly stamped by a smiling clerk, before he hands it back to me and says: 'Welcome to Saudi Arabia.'

I leave the airport. It's nighttime. The temperature is pleasant. I take a taxi to the hotel I've booked in advance. Looking out the window, Riyadh at first sight seems like an intermittent city; blinding lights alternate with dark streets with no buildings whatsoever. The touching of two extremes: total fullness immediately followed by the emptiness of air. There isn't a soul on the streets. Cars shoot by. Forty minutes later we reach the hotel in Batha, in the city's historic centre, an area the Saudis consider disreputable and generally steer clear of. All around me are Asian immigrants, all men. 'Welcome to Saudi Arabia,' I think to myself, before heading off to bed.

After a sleep interrupted by the muezzin from the mosque beside my hotel, which shook me from my bed at five in the morning, I get ready to go and attend the conference. This is an important meeting, including several African heads of state, various ministers from the host kingdom and other Gulf nations, officials of differing kinds and rank, and businessmen intent on establishing useful contacts for the future. It is held in one of Riyadh's luxury hotels, which is practically a city in itself, so much so that my taxi driver insists on knowing which entrance I need to go to. 'There's a big difference,' he answers when I tell him I have no idea. 'If you go in through the wrong entrance, you risk walking around inside for a couple of kilometres.' On the way to the hotel we pass some of the city's landmark buildings: the Kingdom Tower, 300 metres tall and with an enormous orifice between the upper floors that has led more malicious observers to nickname it 'the bottle opener'; the Ministry for Internal Affairs, a sort of inverted double pyramid with tiny windows that looks like a spaceship just descended upon the city; and the Al Faisaliah Tower with its slightly less salubrious glass globe on top that houses an exclusive restaurant. All ultramodern buildings deliberately designed to flaunt their opulence and extravagance. They are projected towards the future, as if in deliberate contrast to the ultraconservative nature of a country in which women are not allowed to drive or work in jobs that involve contact with men. The impression they give the world is: 'We are traditionalists, but we are not primitive. We don't let our women drive or work, but we send them shopping in the most sparkling shopping centres on the planet.' Built to amaze, these structures stand out in a city that is otherwise fairly anonymous: a maze of three-lane roads without pedestrians; commercial centres, service stations, and fast food restaurants where the food comes directly from machines. Born out of nothing in the centre of a desert plain, Riyadh developed horizontally: the distances are monstrous, and the total lack of public transport services means that the streets are constantly clogged, especially since fuel is practically free here. Moving from one part of the city to another often requires infinite patience, not least because the taxi drivers – who are almost all Bengali, Pakistani or Indian – only know the major reference points and therefore can't extricate themselves from the main thoroughfares.

Fortunately, the hotel where the conference is being held is one of those well-known reference points, and we get there without any trouble. It is truly enormous, sprawling over at least two square kilometres, with dozens of entrances marked in sequence by letters. Each entrance is protected by a security block with armed guards who check the cars with metal detectors. After walking through the security gate, I ask for directions to the 'Gulf-Africa Investment Conference', and learn that although I have used the wrong entrance I am not too far away. Finding my way through a series of interconnecting corridors, I eventually come upon the hall where the conference is being held. It has a range of display stands: one for the

Saudi Chamber of Commerce, one for the Islamic Development bank, and another for the Binladin Group which, although possessing a nefarious reputation in the West, is one of the leading private Saudi groups and is involved in the new wave of agricultural investment.[14] The hall is large with a coffered ceiling and enormous glass lamps that illuminate it even in daytime. It is filled with a mixed group of Saudis in their traditional white *dishdashas* and Africans in suits and ties. There are a few western journalists, and a small number of women, grouped together in one area slightly off to one side. For this occasion, a partial exception has been made to the kingdom's strict segregation rules, which normally dictate that women on their own must never be in a room where men are present. Here they have been seated in an area apart from the men and yet remain visible. Only during lunch is the normal system of division reinforced: once they have queued with the men for the buffet, they are invited to sit at tables at the end of the restaurant, protected from prying eyes by wooden partitions.

The conference begins with the ritual thanking of King Abdullah, who is presently undergoing a delicate surgery in the United States. After the best wishes for a speedy recovery and various forms of *salamelecchi*, the interventions by the many institutions begin. Speeches are given by Saudi ministers, and by African heads of state and other officials. The talks underline that what is being celebrated here is a great opportunity to strengthen a partnership created through friendship, mutual respect and reciprocal opportunity. All are in agreement that African nations and those of the Gulf Cooperation Council (GCC)[15] must interweave new commercial relations and establish successful synergies.

The theme of the plenary session is very general in scope. A number of speakers provide figures relating to the degree of commercial exchange between their nations and those in the

Gulf, while others limit themselves to expressing declarations of intent. Although the investments under discussion relate to various sectors, it is almost immediately clear that the focus of the meeting is on agriculture. One crystal clear example of this comes when the plenary session is followed by four 'work groups': 'commerce', 'telecommunications and infrastructure', 'energy, minerals and natural resources', and 'agriculture'. Whereas the first three are held in relatively confined spaces, in which participants are grouped almost informally around tables, the fourth takes place in a large conference hall, fully equipped for simultaneous translation into Arabic, English and French. Well before this meeting begins, the room is full. Soon it is standing room only. At the speakers' table sit managers from Saudi Arabia and the other Gulf States, officials from large international organisations – especially the World Bank and FAO – and African ministers. The floor is given to the Saudis who immediately emphasise their foreign leasing policy and KAISAIA. Their Vice-Minister for Agriculture, Abdullah Al Obaid, defines it as a 'philanthropic initiative' aimed at increasing the agricultural productivity of the countries concerned and at creating development. 'It is a natural partnership: on the one hand there is an abundance of land, water and labour; on the other a surplus of capital.' Without going into too much detail, he describes his government's involvement, from supplying credit to private investors to facilitating rental agreements with the selected countries. The latter must have certain fundamental characteristics: in particular, good relations with the kingdom, and infrastructure suitable for the transport and exportation of agricultural produce. In addition, they mustn't place limits on exports or conditions on the type of produce grown. After briefly describing how the process works, the vice-minister affirms that the plan launched by King Abdullah offers nothing but benefits and, in a sort of *excusatio non petita*, underlines that 'our programme is complementary and is not in competition with local production'. He concludes with a statement intended as a justification but that sounds like an admission of guilt by a *reo confesso*: 'This is an old phenomenon. The Gulf States are only doing now what the Europeans have done for years.'

Nobody in the room seems to bat an eyelid at this blatant confession of neo-colonialism. Not a trace of a murmur or a grumble, only smiles and approval. The vice-minister's speech is met with a hearty round of applause, and the floor is given to José Pacheco, Mozambique's Minister for Agriculture. About fifty, well dressed, he is one of the new Directors of Frelimo, the party that arose from Marxist guerrillas and has held on to the reins of power since 1975, the year in which the country won its independence from Portugal. Pacheco was Minister for Internal Affairs until a few weeks ago, when he was moved to Agriculture. The violent reaction by the police to protests over the high cost of living – which had exploded a few months previously following a hike in the price of bread, and which ended in the deaths of thirteen people – cost him his Internal Affairs position. He had already been involved in agriculture for many years, having trained as an agronomist and held the position of vice-minister in a previous government. From his behaviour in his new role, it would appear he hasn't learnt a thing from the revolts, which were essentially caused by his country's dependence on food imports despite its extraordinary agricultural potential. Pacheco seems convinced that this potential should be placed in the hands of foreign investors, even if this policy risks dwindling even further the prospects for his nation's self-sufficiency for food. After thanking the participants and the organisers, the minister launches into a presentation with the aid of a big screen. He presents – for the lesser prepared – a map of Mozambique, complete with general geographical indicators such as its borders, population, landscape. He puts up a few photos, obviously intended to show the luxuriant nature of the environment, 'suitable for many different kinds of cultivations'. He points out that his government has recently taken various initiatives aimed at facilitating foreign investment, 'creating a favourable economic environment'. He then goes on to describe these initiatives in detail: the abolition of duties on the importation of machinery; the fast-tracking of licensing procedures for investors; no cap on the exportation of food produce, and so on. He talks about fifty-year rental agreements, renewable for another fifty years. Then comes a dramatic pause before he reveals his next slide, which he believes will deliver the knockout punch, the information that will win over the undecided among the audience. He clicks on the mouse to bring up a table detailing the rental charges: vast regions of land are on offer at one dollar a hectare. 'This is our price because we believe in shared development', affirms Pacheco in an assured tone, as he expounds on the magnificence of the progressive outcome of 'a new green revolution that we must launch together to enter into the new millennium'. He sounds more like a street speaker than a minister. His speech is aimed less at describing his country's potential than at convincing those listening to buy it. Everything he says is driven by one objective: to persuade his audience to come to Mozambique and cultivate land, which his government has undertaken to provide for them at a pittance. The government he speaks of and for has come in force to Riyadh – during the plenary session his President, Armando Guebuza, spoke more generally but in a similar fashion, demonstrating a strong desire to become a privileged partner, to show the Saudis and the other Arab states that Mozambique is open for business, wide open to foreign investors who wish to rent land. The rulers from Maputo want to make ground, having fallen behind in the pecking order: their country is not on the list of those visited by the KAISAIA team. Due to a lack of previous contacts, language difficulties, or whatever other reasons, Mozambique was not among those initially taken into consideration. The delegation from Maputo wants to put this initial mistake right.

But the competition is fierce. As soon as Pacheco is finished and the discussion opened up to those in the hall, a man in his forties leaps up from the first row to ask for a chance to speak. He introduces himself. He is an official from Ethiopia's Ministry for Rural Development, and works in the same investment agency that I had visited in Addis Ababa. 'Our country is also happy to welcome foreign investors in agriculture', he says, before adding conscientiously, 'our minister would have gladly come to this conference, but for an organisational oversight.' In other words, he probably wasn't officially invited. Having picked this particular bone, the man goes on to basically repeat what Esayas Kebede, his office manager, had told me a few weeks before. Some of his rhetoric is exactly the same as that used by his boss: his country has an enormous abundance of water and cultivable land, its climate permits several harvests per year, and 'three million hectares have been put on the market'. He talks about the abolition of duties on the importation of machinery and the possibility of exporting all of the produce cultivated. Immediately after, as if wanting to cancel blow-for-blow the affirmations from the minister from Mozambique, he says that the Ethiopians are renting land for even less: 'Depending on the location, we can even rent at 70 to 50 cents in dollars per hectare.' He would also like to make a PowerPoint presentation, but is interrupted by the moderator, who gives the floor to a fat man with a drooping jaw and an elegant suit that is having trouble containing him. The man introduces himself as a minister from the Central African Republic. 'Our country is landlocked, and has no access to the sea. But it has an enormous supply of water. We have millions of hectares of uncultivated land and we would be more than happy to give it to foreign investors who are capable of utilising it.' One of the world's poorest countries, torn apart by continual coups and an infrastructure system so lacking that it almost defies belief, even the Central African Republic is on the market. A market whose prices continue to fall. 'For the first to avail themselves of this opportunity, we are prepared to make a particular concession', declares the minister in a baritone voice that seems to come from the pit of his diaphragm. 'For a period to be defined, we will give them the land completely free of charge.'

Qatar, the Emir's dream

'That auction in the hall was a sorry spectacle' – Mahendra Shah doesn't mince his words when commenting upon the work group in which he has just taken part. This sixty-year-old Indian, raised in Kenya and educated at Cambridge, is the Director of the Qatar National Food Security Programme. Slim, not very tall, with piercing eyes, Shah is the quintessential global official. He worked for years for the World Bank, FAO and other United Nations agencies before being called by the Emir of Qatar to run his new programme on food security, a top priority for the small and arid Gulf state. His arrival at Doha is a further example of Hamad bin Khalifa Al Thani's modern and pragmatic nature, following upon the information giant that is the Al Jazeera satellite channel. With a lot of money but not much home-grown expertise, the Emir has adopted a winning tactic across many different sectors: to attract some of the best experts from around the world. And Shah is undoubtedly a hard hitter: brilliant, competent, not prone to using the soft tones of diplomacy. 'The giving away of land that we saw in there is disgusting', he repeats, as we sit talking over a post-lunch coffee in two armchairs outside the conference hall. Before getting down to the subject in hand, he tells me about his Italian past, which isn't limited to his years at FAO. 'When I was at university in England, I was going out with a girl from Milan,' he says. 'Her brother, Elio, used to come to visit her quite often. The boy was a force of nature, a volcano of ideas. One day he decided to talk me into a business venture with him: we would buy some pants that he would then take over to sell in Italy. "These are perfect for the prostitutes back in Milan," he said. I wasn't convinced but I followed his lead, and put some money into the deal. It turned out that his instincts were spot-on: when he got to Italy, Elio sold all the pants in two days flat. And so he bought more. And then more again. The little venture started to make a decent profit. So he proposed setting up a real business, for which we would be full partners. I turned him down, told him I wanted to continue my academic career. Now if I had said yes, I'd probably be a billionaire by now, as founding member of one of the world's biggest clothing brands: Elio Fiorucci,' he says, laughing.

Shah is a man of the world. He's lived in half the planet. He's moved with ease from the West to Africa and Asia, without looking down on the occasional relaxing break at the wellness centre he owns in Bali. His role in the Qatar project is Director General for foreign investment. And from what he says, it appears that he has quite a free rein there. His vision, which he succinctly expressed during the work group, is different from that of the Saudis. He doesn't propose accords with governments, but rather more stable partnerships with the farmers. 'Governments come and go, farmers stay – they're the ones we should work with.' He's probably been put off by an agreement that he negotiated with the Kenyan government, which offered land to Qatar in return for the building of a commercial port in the city of Lamu. Denounced by several organisations from Kenyan civil society, the agreement was cancelled. 'There were problems. I don't think the project's going to go ahead', he says without offering further details.[16] Some of the things he had said during his presentation made me want to meet him: Shah hadn't spoken about land rentals, but about joint ventures between Gulf investors and African farmers. He'd talked about a balanced approach, in which increases in production should be shared between exportation and local consumption. He'd talked about the transfer of expertise. Basically, he'd presented ideas that were more original than those of the Saudis.

Besides investing in the advanced desalination techniques and intensive cultivation that are compatible with the small size of the country, the programme Shah manages 'proposes to create an integrated system that works for everybody'. He presents his project with the enthusiasm commonly found in a visionary: 'We put in the capital, the farmers provide the land and the labour. If we produce 500, 200 is exported to Qatar, 200 goes to the farmers and 100 is sold in the local market. The proceeds from this last part are reinvested to increase productivity.' The idea, a sort of large-scale version of contract farming,[17] is enormously ambitious, and Shah makes no bones about this. 'In a couple of years, we can become a hub, a centre for agricultural production that can export to China and India.'

In spite of Shah's confidence, the question that springs to mind is simply this: is such a project really sustainable? Were it to be fully implemented, there's little doubt that it would benefit all concerned. But is it actually possible in Africa to make agreements with the farmers while bypassing their governments? In almost all African countries, the land is the property of the state and is cultivated by farmers on a common law basis. Who is the counter-party in an agreement of this kind? The government of the country involved? The associations that represent the farmers, in those places where they actually exist? The village chiefs? 'Our objective', says Shah, 'is to involve everybody concerned, by making them understand that the benefit is collective. We provide the money to increase production. The land remains in the hands of those who have always used it. All we ask for is a fair share of what is produced.' The project is still in an embryonic state. The first contacts have been made, but as yet nothing has been set in motion. Shah's presence in Riyadh is part of a general public relations strategy, and is bearing fruit: on the fringes of the conference, the Vice-President of Ghana, John Dramani Mahama, is announcing to journalists that his government is negotiating with Qatar over the creation of a joint venture to produce food for both countries. While Mahama talks, surrounded by microphones and television cameras, at the end of the room Shah nonchalantly sips on his tea, observing the scene from afar, enjoying the first small signs of success for an idea that he believes is destined for a radiant future.

'Business is an adventure'

I'm visiting the 'second house' of Faisal bin Abdulaziz Albeshr. It's a sort of tent-shaped prefabricated building in the garden of a villa, with carpets throughout and a TV tuned into an English Premier League football match. 'I come here to rest and talk with my friends,' he says as he meets me at the door, offering a vigorous handshake and a large, welcoming smile. Faisal is the president of a company that has been in business in Sudan for the past eight years, and this is why I've come to meet him. He's got deep black eyes and a long beard that forks out at the sides. He's not particularly tall, and robust without being fat. His expression conveys a firm intelligence. After the pleasantries he invites me into his tent. The surroundings are very quiet – the house beside the garden where he has raised his annex is unoccupied. 'Every now and then it's rented for the weekend,' he tells me after I've spent ten minutes wandering around the maze of rooms looking for a bathroom.

If there's one thing Riyadh certainly doesn't have it's an accommodation problem. There are plenty of houses and they are usually enormous: Abdullah, a friend of a close friend of mine who has offered to show me around the city, says that his apartment, consisting of six rooms for him, his wife and their newborn child, is 'a bit small'. Wang Junpeng, a Chinese journalist sent here for four years as a correspondent (and who was already on the verge of a nervous breakdown after just four months) told me that, before arriving, he rented a 'medium-sized' house, only to be presented with a three-floor villa complete with pool which he shares with his wife. 'Sometimes, when we call each other from one room to the next, we can hear an echo,' he says with a mixture of amusement and anguish.

In a country almost devoid of a public dimension, and where men – and even more so women – spend a large part of their time in their own properties, it's almost natural that houses here assume an importance which differs greatly from what they mean in the West. Any Saudi worth his salt has at least two houses in the city, and if he doesn't have a second he will rent one every so often. To give me an idea of the scale of the phenomenon, Abdullah takes me to a district a long way from the centre, near the desert on the outskirts of the city. It's an area full of villas surrounded by walls and iron gates. He stops the car in front of one, and knocks on the gate. A guard opens the gate and leads us past a small garden to the house, which is roughly 300 square metres and furnished in a fairly nondescript fashion. It's hard to tell how many rooms there are. 'People rent these places for the weekend. Sometimes they bring their family here to relax. Or they organise parties, away from the prying eyes of the *muttawa*, the religious police.' In a society where relations with the opposite sex before marriage are banned, and which lacks even the most basic forms of entertainment (no cinemas, obviously no discos, and the only bars are Starbucks or similar franchises in the commercial centres which have guards banning single boys from entering, for fear they might hook up with girls via BlackBerry), everything happens behind domestic closed doors. Some go to their second homes to meet their friends, some to engage in illicit behaviour (like having sexual relations or drinking alcohol acquired on the black market for a small fortune), others just to take the wife and kids for a weekend break.

Faisal owns his own second house, and he wants me to know that. He's a businessman, and so a second home is a kind of status symbol: 'I come here almost every afternoon, after work.' He's here with his business partner and three old school friends. They're having a lively discussion about the game they're watching. The room is bare, which is generally the way with Saudi homes, no decorations on the walls, no furniture. The desire is to reproduce the ambience of a desert tent, even if it is in the garden of a villa in one of Riyadh's residential areas.

Before we begin our interview, Faisal insists I sample a 'little snack' that his wife has prepared. He sets down two trays overflowing with food: one holds enough sandwiches and canapés to feed a small army, the other is filled with vaguely phosphorescent and strangely shaped pastries. I take a couple of sandwiches and ask him about his business. He insists I have more. Then he pours me some coffee and points to another tray with bottles of Coke, Sprite, Fanta. Finally, having satisfactorily met his hospitality obligations, he starts to talk. Faisal is thirty-five and has been working for the past eight years in Sudan, where he has a business that produces potatoes, vegetables and herbal medicines. He tells me that he started to work there almost by chance, on a friend's advice. 'I had some family capital to invest and decided to throw myself into that venture. Up to that point, I didn't know the first thing about agriculture.' He has a land concession of about

15,000 hectares on the banks of the Nile. He produces exclusively for the local market, except for the forage, which he exports to Saudi Arabia. He pays nothing for the land. 'When we started, we were paying 42 dollars an acre.'[18] But after a three-year trial period, our contract was renewed and the rental fee was abolished. They were happy with the way we worked and that we were creating jobs in the region.' He is a shrewd businessman. The land he uses is among the best in all of Sudan. 'All around us now the land is mostly taken by Saudi companies. Nowadays, if you want to rent a plot the annual rent is 1,000 dollars an acre.' Faisal received no help whatsoever from the state. In fact, he says that he refused the risk insurance he was offered by a famous investment bank in Riyadh. 'Business is an adventure which should be lived without parachutes,' he insists. This concept – one that he repeats many times – has influenced his position on his state's policy of support for foreign investment. 'I've heard about it,' he says, in a show of boastful indifference. 'But it doesn't interest me. If you want to do business you should be able to accept the risks.' As our talk goes on he gradually starts to express his disapproval at how many people have taken advantage of the king's initiative to do business. 'These people have had a shoe-in. It's a clientele system. I don't like it.'

Faisal is a no-nonsense, full-blooded businessman. He is an entrepreneur primarily interested in profit. He's not particularly attached to the land, even if he regularly goes to check the state of his affairs in Sudan. When he talks about what he grows, it's in a detached tone: 'We grow potatoes and zucchini because they sell better in Sudan. We follow the market.' At the same time, he doesn't want to make money in a parasitical way: the money he makes must be the fruit of his intuition, his nose for business, not due to 'contacts' in this or that Ministry. He is a courageous captain, who has managed to guide his boat with impressive skill, so much so that his business turns a yearly profit of about a million dollars. As an entrepreneur, he is always on the lookout for a new investment. He confesses that he has been asked to enter into a joint venture with a Brazilian group and a Sudanese one to produce ethanol in the African state. I ask him what he knows about agrofuels. 'Little or nothing,' he answers. 'I just want to make money.' I tell him that it's a little strange to see a Saudi investing in alternative fuels to oil. The answer he gives sums up the man, and in a way also encapsulates the split nature and contradictions of this hyper-conservative and yet hyper-modern nation: 'If the opportunity was a good one, I would even go to cultivate land in Israel. Business is business, my friend.'

The critics within KAISAIA

Faisal is not the only one unconvinced by the initiative sponsored by King Abdullah. For differing reasons, a number of agricultural entrepreneurs and influential Saudi personalities are also sceptical. One of these is Fawaz Al Alamy, a former Vice-Minister for Commerce and head of the team that negotiated Saudi Arabia's entrance into the World Trade Organisation (WTO), of which they became full members in 2005. A board member on various state and parastatal bodies, such as Saudi Arabian Airlines and the Saudi Industrial Development Fund, today he is the Director of a consulting firm for multinationals that want to invest in Saudi Arabia. After reading some of his comments on foreign investment, I call him, and he offers to meet me the same morning in his office in the north of Riyadh. He tells me, as is the custom in these parts, to telephone him as soon as I get into the taxi 'so I can explain the route to the driver'. I promptly obey: I leave the hotel, hail a taxi, call him and pass my phone to the Pakistani driver, who listens and nods his head. 'Ten minutes,' he says, using up a significant chunk of the English he knows. He slips the car in gear and sets off confidently. The city rolls by. All the streets seem the same, but after a while I get the vague sensation that we're going around in circles. After twenty minutes, we're still very much in the car. My phone rings. It's Fawaz. 'Where are you?' he asks. 'I don't know.' 'Let me talk to the driver.' Fresh directions follow, more nods of the head, and a final 'ok, no problem' which doesn't reassure me in the least. The driver reverses the taxi and sets off in the opposite direction. I look at him inquisitively. 'Do you know where to go?' 'No problem,' he repeats. This time he seems more assured. We set off at speed without a hint of hesitation. My mind turns to the questions I want to ask Al Alamy. The city flows by past my window. I'm busy writing a few notes on my pad when the driver pulls over.

'What's happening?' I ask him. 'Call the man,' he responds in a tone that says it all. I call Fawaz, who shows the first signs of irritation. I'm afraid he's going to cancel our appointment; he's been waiting for me for at least forty minutes. The two men talk on the phone, and the previous scene is re-enacted, complete with the 'ok, no problem' at the end. The driver sets off again. I don't know what to think. The city rolls on. The taxi driver drives. The fee on the taximeter is extravagantly high. I'm just about to tell him to return to the hotel when my phone rings again. It's Al Alamy. 'Tell the driver to stop. I can see you from my window. You've just passed my office.'

The office is in a single-floor building, modern, bright, windows everywhere. Two men at the reception ask me to wait in the conference room next door, a large room with two elegant leather sofas, a desk at the end and plain white walls. Fawaz arrives five minutes later and introduces himself by handing me his business card, which is a masterpiece of sobriety: a small white card with the simple inscription 'Fawaz Al Alamy – consultant' and an email address. This little detail wins me over – in a world in which everybody is clambering to have a defined role and belong to a specific group, someone who presents himself with the vague title of 'consultant' has something of the rebel or unapologetic anti-conformist about him. He's not tall, he has a small grey split moustache and a sharp gaze that softens every so often as his eyes open wide, almost as if to capture the attention of whoever is talking to him. He does it quite a lot when discussing his business activity. 'I'm working on a big project, which will be concluded over the next few months,' he tells me. He then starts to show me a presentation on a big screen. A series of tables appear which demonstrate what I have been hearing for days: that Saudi Arabia has a desperate need to assure food security for itself and that, given its lack of water reserves, it cannot rely solely on its own forces. 'We must guarantee for ourselves an adequate system of supplies and storage.' The company he is setting up – and whose business plan he shows me on the screen, underlining that this information is 'confidential' – has the aim of establishing itself as a distributor of primary foodstuffs produced elsewhere, by virtue of selective agreements with large agribusiness companies (such as the American firm Cargill). It's a more classic strategy than the one launched by King Abdullah. But according to Al Alamy it is also more secure. To explain the concept better he uses a medical metaphor: 'A patient on dialysis must guarantee for himself permanent access to a hospital in order to receive his treatment. Otherwise he will die.' Al Alamy doesn't openly criticise the king, but he clearly implies that KAISAIA runs the risk of being the wrong treatment for a patient who is chronically short of food and water, that patient being Saudi Arabia. 'According to the rules of the World Trade Organisation, every nation can decide to block exports if necessary.' 'And so', he adds with a touch of cynicism, 'it could happen that you find yourself undercutting produce locally for which you have paid a lot to trade elsewhere.' The man speaks from experience. A few years ago, he helped some Saudi and Kuwaiti entrepreneurs set up a sugar refinery in Sudan. 'We invested an enormous sum, but we never saw a single kilo of sugar. The Sudanese didn't let us export.'

In light of this, Al Alamy describes the king's programme as 'too risky'. 'Personally, I wouldn't invest a cent,' he says, emphasising his words with a raise of his eyebrows and a sharpening of his gaze. In his opinion, the kingdom shouldn't be investing in land around the world, but in a much more efficient system of storage, both of primary food produce and water resources – which should be increased through further investment in desalination technology. These systems should, according to his personal vision, be developed together with the other GCC states, who all share the same problems as Saudi Arabia but, 'surprisingly', act in an autonomous way, 'without cooperating with each other'.

I hear many of the same criticisms almost verbatim from Turki Faisal Al Rasheed, the Director of Golden Grass, a company that has been involved in agriculture since the 1980s. Al Rasheed is a fairly unusual character for Saudi Arabia. He's actively involved with his own foundation for the advancement of democracy, a decidedly ambitious objective in a country that is an absolute monarchy of tribal ancestry. He is an occasional columnist for a number of the kingdom's newspapers, in which he speaks about human rights, elections and the prospects for agriculture. On this last point, the one that interests me the most, I read an interesting piece of his in which he defended subsidies for agriculture, arguing that it is actually 'the farmer who subsidises the state because he guarantees it a minimum level of food security'.

When I call him, he is so willing and courteous that he even sends his personal secretary to pick me up at my hotel. 'We wanted to spare you the difficult experience of driving around in circles trying to find us,' says Ronnie, his Filipino assistant, who has a chubby face, a purple shirt that clashes violently with his blue tie, and thirty years of experience in a country 'that you end up getting used to'. After asking me where I come from, Ronnie asks if I am a Catholic. I tell him that I'm not really interested in religion, and he is visibly disappointed. Perhaps he wanted to establish an empathy based on a shared faith. Or maybe it just seems absurd to him that someone could candidly say that they're not interested in religion in a place where religion shapes every single aspect of life, from male-female relationships to the opening hours of shops, which close for half an hour every time the muezzin calls the masses to prayer.

When I arrive at Golden Grass's headquarters, I meet Al Rasheed as he's heading to the mosque for one of the five daily worships. Slender and elegantly dressed in a green tunic, with an impeccably manicured beard framing a smooth, linear face, he asks me to kindly wait for him in his waiting room. Ronnie shows me the way, brings me a coffee, and turns the TV on to a football match. I look around and study the manager's photos: in one he is heading a delegation of electoral observers in Bahrain, in another he is at a reception party in the presence of one of the Saudi princes, another is presumably an end-of-year school photo. After about twenty minutes, Al Rasheed reappears and shows me into his office. We sit on the sofa. His English is extremely refined. He studied in Liverpool, and his years in the United Kingdom not only gave him a perfect mastery of English but also a very European tendency not to waste time but to get to the point. So we skip the small talk and go straight to the interview. As we talk, he is interrupted every so often by his staff, who bring him cheques and other documents to sign. 'You must excuse me,' he says. 'I only returned from Europe yesterday, and I'm afraid I have a considerable amount of work to catch up on.'

On foreign investment, Al Rasheed shares much of the perplexity expressed by Al Alamy. 'It's not safe. Who is going to guarantee that the contracts won't be reviewed and that the host country won't suddenly ban you from exporting?' He points out that those who have taken part thus far are people linked to the royal family or to consolidated networks in the countries in which they are investing. 'Take Al Amoudi, for example. He is half Ethiopian and, as is well known, enjoys a particular rapport with the party in power and with the Prime Minister in Addis Ababa. His investment is relatively safe. But how can this be said for others? I believe that an operation of this kind can only work if the land is bought. Rents can always be revoked.' Al Rasheed predicts that in the end not many groups will subscribe to King Abdullah's initiative. 'There are no hard-and-fast rules. I don't understand how such a thing could work.'

'So how can Saudi Arabia guarantee food security then?' I ask him.

'I believe', he responds, 'that the government should work on two fronts: one local and one international, to assure diversified provisions for its people but without leasing directly.' His view of the international front basically echoes that of Al Alamy: agreements with agribusiness companies to obtain the grain, corn, barley and rice necessary for internal consumption. But it is his comments on the so-called 'local front' that show the most original aspect of the manager's thinking on the subject. Al Rasheed shows himself to have a comprehensive and multi-functional vision of agriculture: 'The government cannot totally abandon the farmers, because agriculture has a social function. If the state doesn't invest in rural communities, they will become depopulated, as people will move to the cities. Such a development inevitably leads to increases in urban poverty, crime and prostitution.'

Al Rasheed then tells me that I needn't look too far to understand his argument. 'This is one of the principal reasons why France, Germany and the European Union in general subsidise agriculture to the tune of millions of euros. Nobody wants to see their countryside transformed into a stream of phantom villages. This is the risk that we are running in Saudi Arabia. Empty countrysides, interspersed with the occasional mega-business, and crowded cities, full of unemployment and abject misery.'

Herds of cattle in the middle of the desert

The countryside I see through the car window as I travel from Riyadh to Kharj not only seems depopulated but totally unsuitable for a stable settlement: not many would aspire to living in an endless stretch of sand. Only when I get nearer the town and the landscape becomes less brushy, softened by green bushes and date palm trees, do I understand what Al Rasheed was saying: many of the businesses that line this road were founded and survive because of subsidies. I haven't come to visit the settlements in the Saudi countryside, however, but to see the Almarai plant: 'the largest integrated dairy farm in the world', according to the brochure I was given the day before at their office in Riyadh.

'We'll be there in twenty kilometres,' says my bored Bengalese driver, while we are talking about the subject most in vogue in Saudi Arabia: sex. Completely repressed in public society, banned by law outside marriage, it's not surprising that people talk of little else. Amal is telling me about the exclusive parties in very private villas at which everything is permitted. He says that nothing is found wanting: there is alcohol, women who are 'open to everything', even 'whatever drug you desire, my friend'. He says he knows the right people to get invited ('for the right price', which I learn is exorbitant). I can't tell if he's a pathological liar or a kind of pimp who has found his own particular niche in Saudi Arabia. The car we are travelling in, a brand-new black Mercedes, is his own, which places him quite a few rungs higher up the social ladder than those of his compatriots who drive rented taxis for an average wage of 50 riyals a day (about 10 euros). I decide not to investigate further. My eyes focus on the road ahead: one long endless stretch. A blue signpost with white writing indicates Almarai, 20 kilometres.

The company produces milk, cheese, yoghurt. It follows the line all the way through, from the grazing cow to the packaged product. It was created in 1976 as an initiative of Prince Sultan bin Mohammad bin Saud Al Kabeer. This was the period in which the royal family decided that the country shouldn't be importing milk and its derivatives, and so resolved to provide whatever was necessary to fill this void. State petrodollars were invested to set up what were to become in the space of a few years the two giants of dairy production in the Middle East: Almarai and Al Safi, the latter managed until his death by Prince Mohammad bin Abdullah Al Faysal, a man with such an ambitious outlook that at the height of his creative vision he wanted to guarantee the country's water supply by dragging icebergs down from the North Pole. Both Al Safi and Almarai were created from nothing; there were no animals, the water was buried deep in the ground, the land a sandbox. With the financial clout that only the Saudis can swing, thousands of heads of cattle were transported from the United States and Latin America. Ultra-modern technology was used to dig down into the depths of the earth and draw water to the surface. Today the countryside around the company farms is awash with green and yellow: the desert has made way for cultivation and a blaze of agricultural businesses that have sprung up to exploit the water beneath the ground.

The Almarai farm is as big as an urban conglomerate: it spreads out as far as the eye can see, a massive complex of sheds where the cattle are kept. I am met at the gate by John, a manager from Ireland, a red-faced man with the body of a fighter which is just beginning to show signs of stoutness. He starts by driving me around, but with each question it becomes clearer that he's keeping his distance. When I ask him what it's like to live in Saudi Arabia, playing on the common chord of our European heritage, he responds that it's not bad and that the work is interesting. I have another go, pointing out that 'here is a little different to his green isle'. He nods his head. So I change tack and focus on his profession: 'It must be a lot harder to raise cattle here than in Ireland.' 'A fair bit', he answers with poetic brevity. I realise that the game is up, and limit myself to asking him about the company, to which he responds with a surprising wealth of detail.

The cattle are part of a veritable industrial system. Housed in air-conditioned stalls, they are milked three times a day, every eight hours. Each milking takes between five and seven minutes, depending on the quality of the milk. The animals are organised into real and proper batteries which continuously substitute each other. As their milk is pumped through their udders, ultra-modern machinery calculates its quality, analysing its acidity level, and detecting the presence of any impurities. Other machinery, in another area of the farm, measures the nutrition percentage in the forage. Everything is computerised: the feed is a mixture of alfalfa, barley, corn and grain combined in precise proportions aimed at maximising productivity. 'We have 20,000 tonnes of feed in stock,' says the Irishman. 'Some of it we produce ourselves, the rest we buy in.'

It's hot outside, but not roasting. It's the middle of winter and the thermometer reads 25 degrees. 'But summer can get a little tough,' admits John. 'It can go higher than fifty degrees. Even the cows suffer and their production falls.' On average for the year, each cow produces roughly forty litres of milk per day. Between this farm and the surrounding ones that together make up the Almarai production plant there are 80,000 cattle, so the average total production is about three million litres of milk per day.

The complex where the milk, cheese and yoghurt are produced is a few kilometres away. Here, extremely powerful machinery filters the liquid, refines it and renders it ready for consumption. The production plant is so vast that we have to drive everywhere to get around. Outside, a fleet of trucks is waiting to take the finished products not just to Saudi tables but throughout the Gulf States. 'We are the leading dairy business in the region, with twelve thousand employees,' I am proudly told by the Communications Manager, Majed Al Doyhi, a man of about thirty with an elongated face, a tidy goatee and slightly Asian eyes.

As I listen to his words and the head-spinning figures he reels off, I look around at all the machinery, the trucks, the cattle panting in the sheds, and am even more convinced than before that the Saudis feel obliged to do things big. What else could explain the importation of tens of thousands of cattle into this harsh and hostile environment which is so clearly unsuitable for an enterprise of this kind? And the Saudis don't just want to be big. They want to be the best. Within a twenty kilometre range of here there are three complexes worthy of the Guinness Book of Records: between Almarai and Al Safi, who are fighting it out between themselves for the title of biggest dairy farm in the world, there is also Prince Sultan's Air Base, which at 100 square kilometres is the largest on the planet. This, I think to myself, is the true essence of Saudi Arabia: a country of excesses, where everything is possible, even herds of cattle grazing in the middle of the desert.

LAND GRABBING

A tonne of produce in a square metre of water
A few dozen kilometres from the Almarai mega-farm, a small plot of land unfolds by the side of an unmarked dirt road. A small path leads to a clearing where there are two prefabricated hovels. The clearing is surrounded by vegetable fields. There's a shed filled with sheep, and some containers about twenty metres away. 'This is the future. Not all that land abroad nonsense,' says the engineer Mofareh Aljahbli, pointing at the metal structures. The man welcomes me in the shack that serves as his office: there's a wooden table with an ancient computer covered in dust, a tattered old sofa and a couple of armchairs. He offers me tea and, together with his Egyptian Project Manager, tells me about his hydroponics technology. 'It has an incredible yield. We can produce a ton of forage in a square metre of water in just one week. We only started last January and we're already raking in profits.' The containers lying on one side of his plot are his hen that lays the golden eggs. 'At the beginning there were two, then four. Now we have eight, and we want to expand more.'

After deluging me with a wealth of technical information, he takes me to see the containers. Inside, there are stacks of plastic basins filled with seeds. The circulation of water and the humidity of the environment cause the seeds to germinate at an incredible speed. 'The product is ready in one week.' The basins are placed on various shelves according to what day their production started: and there really are seven levels of shelves. Every day the basins are moved up one level higher. When they reach the top level, the plants are ready. At this point, the contents are removed: an extremely dense block of forage. The engineer takes it to the animal shed, places it in the sheep's trough, and they finish it off in a matter of minutes. 'It's very nutritional,' the man tells me with a pleased look on his face, as he watches his animals bleat happily.

Hydroponics is the cultivation of seeds without earth, in a solution of highly nutritional salts which develop the plants at high speed. Given that the amount of water needed for this type of cultivation is approximately a twentieth of the amount required for the same degree of production in a field, this technique may well prove an excellent solution for a country as lacking in water as Saudi Arabia is. But the technique is not taking off: according to Aljahbli, his is the only firm of its kind in the entire kingdom. The company produces a relatively modest quantity of produce and only sells to livestock farms around Kharj. The government hasn't shown much interest in the venture thus far. 'The Minister for Agriculture came here, said he was enthusiastic about the project. But I haven't heard from him since.'

So why doesn't Saudi Arabia adopt this technique on a large scale, given that it would enable an increase in production without wasting the country's scarce and precious supply of water? Why are all efforts being concentrated on the acquisition of land abroad, which is more costly and carries greater risks? The engineer has his explanation for the royal family's lack of enthusiasm. In his opinion, it is all due to a conflict of interest arising from the existence of 'extremely strong ties between certain government members and the leading producer of fertiliser, whose profits would fall if hydroponics was to become more widespread'. Maybe Aljahbli is right: it's nothing more than a story of ordinary corruption, of passing envelopes or favours that certain powerful people must return. Looking at his rusty containers, however, another possibility comes to mind. Hydroponics has one main drawback: it's not visible enough. It doesn't have any of the qualities that excite the Riyadh government. It doesn't amaze. It doesn't send any message to the world. It isn't grandiose like the fields of grain that shine in the desert, or the mega-complexes of Al Safi or Almarai, or the Kingdom Tower in Riyadh, or the increasingly vast and hyper-technological cultivations that the Saudis are setting up in Africa. Empty spaces and a mania for enormity: these seem to me to be the essence of Saudi Arabia. These, and an almost endless supply of funds. Never mind hydroponics – it occurs to me that if it applies its elephantine syndrome and spending power to KAISAIA, Riyadh is going to end up sucking in millions of hectares of farmable land in Africa.

CHAPTER 3

Geneva: The Financiers of Arable Land

The FAO building in Rome, 13 October 2010. It's eleven o'clock on a rainy morning in early autumn. In the central hall of the building that houses the Food and Agriculture Organisation of the United Nations, the tables at the small internal bar are half empty. The stands of various organisations on display a few metres away are all deserted. The row of online computers put at the disposal of the delegates is an uninterrupted series of empty chairs and motionless screens. The important summit on food security that I've come to follow doesn't seem to have captured the imagination: my press badge says number six, despite the fact that I got it the day after the summit began. I head for the bar and order a coffee. The barman prepares it for me. 'Slow day?' he asks me, sensing my disappointment at the lifeless atmosphere that surrounds us. I smile. Neither he nor I have the slightest notion that something strange is about to happen within the next five minutes.

As I slowly sip my coffee to pass a little time, a group of people arrive who look much different to the officials in suits and ties wandering around the corridors. There are about twenty of them. They are wearing traditional shirts, bandanas around their necks, red and green T-shirts. I feel a certain excitement as I watch them set up. From a bag they pull out two banners. Then they line up at the sides of the hall and unfurl the banners. White writing on a green background, one in Italian and one in English. 'Land grabbing causes hunger. Let small farmers feed the world.' Two men and two women move away from the group and four lecterns are produced: Africa is drawn on one, Latin America on another, then Europe and Asia. Each of the four place the continent they are representing behind them. Then they introduce themselves: an Indonesian, Henry Saragih; a Congolese, Hortense Kinkodila; a Brazilian, Conceiçaõ Muora; and an Italian, Antonio Pozzi. They are representing farming organisations from half the planet. As they speak, a man in a dark suit with a cigar in his mouth approaches from the end of the hall. Sellotaped to his jacket are slips of paper with handwritten inscriptions: Daewoo, Deutsche Bank, Morgan Stanley, Goldman Sachs. The well-dressed man goes up to them with a sheet of paper in his hand, and offers it to them. It's a land lease proposal. The four give him filthy looks. Then, one by one, they speak up.

Henry says: 'In Indonesia, land grabbing is nothing new, because it already happened during colonisation. Nonetheless, new institutions such as the World Bank and the International Monetary Fund are pushing our governments to privatise and open up to the market. This is a new colonialism.' Hortense takes the tone up a notch: 'In Congo, the government signs agreements with large foreign companies without consulting us. The most fertile land is handed over to agribusiness firms, who convert it into monocultures of jatropha and palm oil for export to Europe.' Her words are echoed by the Brazilian, Conceiçaõ Muora: 'The lifestyles of the farmers are considered primitive. Now, with monocultures, it is assumed that modernity and development have arrived. But the reality is that these monocultures deprive farmers of land, reduce biodiversity, and change the entire territory.' Antonio Pozzi adds a slightly different note: 'In Italy, agricultural land is being transformed into industrial and residential areas. Sabina, near Rome, an agricultural region renowned for the high quality of its oil, is fast becoming a periphery of the capital. Olive trees are being substituted by millions of cubic metres of cement.

And the old farmers are asking themselves: "Now, with all this cement, what are we going to eat?"' At that, all four together rip up the sheet in the face of the elegant man, to the applause of the other participants.

The entire spectacle lasts ten minutes, during which time the hall has been gradually filling up with people. It's as if the unexpected performance has shaken the delegates from their slumber: the tables at the bar are no longer empty. A number of officials are observing the scene, in a mixture of amusement and curiosity. The cloakroom assistants have come out from their corner at the end of the hall to get a better look. The workers who had been silently attaching a red carpet to the floor in anticipation of the arrival of some important dignitary have interrupted their work and are examining the strange and cheerful group with a fair degree of sympathy. The protesters then unfurl another banner that says: 'The land belongs to the farmers.' Someone starts to applaud.

This brief theatrical production, which certainly livened up the meeting of the Committee on World Food Security (CFS),[1] offered a sketchy but nonetheless valuable and effective representation of land grabbing. A gigantic global race, the significance and implications of which have been seen in Ethiopia, in fact extends far beyond that country on the Horn of Africa. The phenomenon is spread out on a planetary scale, with differing ramifications and links, and involves groups and institutions which up until recently were light years away from the simple idea of dedicating themselves to agriculture and the exploitation of land. The protagonists are not only cash-rich governments concerned about increases in the prices of basic foodstuffs, such as the Saudis discussed in the previous chapter. Other entities have also become key players in the race for land: speculative funds, large multinationals, pension funds. All the organisations written on the slips stuck to the hoarder's jacket in the hall at FAO have entered the race. The land is

– in the language of the new investors – a new *asset* in differentiating one's investment portfolio and guaranteeing high returns.

How did it come about that such a tangible and concrete good was transformed into a financial product, and thus became volatile and impalpable? It all started with the stock-market crisis which arose from the collapse of subprime mortgages in the summer of 2007. Immediately after the collapse, many financial market players started to look for new opportunities for making a profit. They began to invest in 'refuge goods' or so-called commodities, from gold to oil, to basic food products such as corn and grain. Their reasoning was simple: The world will continue to eat, and the world's population will continue to grow. Food will become increasingly scarce, and so its price will constantly increase. According to FAO predictions, 'in the next forty years the world's population will increase by 34 percent. Feeding this population will require a 70 percent increase in agricultural production.'² Analysing this from a market point of view – a demand growing exponentially, a supply that is incapable of satisfying it – the deal seems extremely lucrative.

Likewise, the move from investing in commodities to investing in land is an almost automatic one. The corollary of speculating on primary food produce – which only guarantees earnings in the short term and is still susceptible to the rises and falls of the stock market – is investment in land. Hardened groups started to invade the sector. They bought stakes in the exploitation of agricultural land in Brazil, Argentina, Indonesia. The bigger risk-takers went headlong for the African market, which offers fewer guarantees but also the potential for astronomical profits. These funds sometimes operate directly on the ground: they find skilled managers capable of drawing a high yield from the land with industrial-scale cultivations of food produce or biofuels which are then generally exported. Or perhaps they limit themselves to buying equities or shares in funds that have been set up *ad hoc* (the so-called 'private equity funds'), and that invest in agricultural enterprises run by companies that are specialists in the sector. This phenomenon has seen a spectacular growth over the past five years: according to the Spanish NGO, Grain, which runs a website that monitors land acquisition projects throughout the world,[3] from 2007 to the present foreign groups have acquired at least 45 million hectares of land, a size just slightly less than that of Spain. But this data is almost certainly incomplete: agreements are often negotiated in secret, between different governments or between governments and businesses. The terms – rental fee, length of the lease, and various other clauses – rarely come to light. The public in the countries involved often come to learn about it indirectly, by reading the international press, for example. This was the case with the stratospheric agreement that the government of Madagascar signed in 2008 with Daewoo, which saw half the country's arable land ceded for ninety-nine years to the South Korean multinational for the production of corn and palm oil. According to the contract, the land was given free, in return for a promise to create employment and build infrastructure. Uncovered by the *Financial Times*,[4] the deal provoked street protests which in the space of a few weeks brought down Marc Ravalomanana's unpopular government.[5]

The case of Madagascar is an exceptional one, both for the enormity of the agreement and the political consequences it had. In many other countries, the renting or ceding of land is done silently, mostly behind closed doors, between governments looking for strong currencies and investors who either want to make large profits or secure the certainty of being able to import the food they require.

A not very world bank

Initially seen as manna for the agricultural sector in developing countries – which had seen very few investments over the past twenty years – this wind of change is now a source of great concern, both in civil society in the countries affected and among international organisations. It is for this reason that, on this rainy October day, the meeting of the Committee on World Food Security in Rome has assumed a particular relevance. The theme of investment in agriculture and 'land acquisition' – the more diplomatic term for land grabbing – is at the centre of debate. There are officials from various governments. There are experts from FAO and the World Bank. And there are the representatives from farming organisations from all over the world who, with their little play, have made their position on the subject crystal clear.

Their position is explained in detail to me by one of the four angry farmers: Henry Saragih. I go up to introduce myself at the end of the show. He is happy with the performance and the relatively good response from the public. He smiles as he receives compliments and embraces: he seems to have a leadership role among the other activists. Included by the *Guardian* among the 'fifty people who can save the planet',[6] this forty-five-year-old Indonesian has, for the past few years, been the International Coordinator of Via Campesina, a consortium of various peasant movements across the globe. Henry has fought many hard battles: for more than fifteen years his country has been a target for multinationals, who have hoarded enormous tracts of land to grow palm trees for biodiesel production, especially in Sumatra and in the Kalimantan region.[7] As someone who himself has a three-hectare family farm, he has spent many years fighting the transnational companies in an attempt to guarantee access to land for farmers. Together with his colleagues from the Indonesia Peasant Union, he has organised marches and protests, and carried out land occupations. He has built up such a reputation in the empyrean of global militants that the *Guardian* has claimed that the results of his activism 'in the next twenty years will determine if there will still be any rainforest areas intact in Southeast Asia fifty years from now, and will possibly mould the political future of many developing countries'.[8]

With his trademark traditional black cylinder hat, cotton shirt and green bandana, Henry travels like a spinning top around the world, giving voice to the peasants at the large international summits, participating in social forums, and learning about the singular realities that he represents as the coordinator of Via Campesina. He has a sober expression which lights up when he speaks in public. At first glance, his finely trimmed moustache gives him the look of a very pleasant chap, although when talking with him one-to-one you soon find that he can be quite coarse or even brusque. When asked a question, he gives a straight and basic answer, without expanding on the subject. He gets straight to the point. And today his point is this: the land rush is being encouraged by the big international organisations. 'This land grabbing is an integral part of an agribusiness model advanced by institutions such as the World Bank, the International Monetary Fund, the International Fund for Agricultural Development (IFAD), FAO and the European Union. By creating a number of vague principles such as those proposed by the World Bank for "responsible investment in agriculture", these institutions categorically legitimise enormous violations of farmers' rights.' Saragih goes straight to the heart of the problem: having realised the enormous scale of the phenomenon, and having acknowledged that in many cases farmers have been removed from their own land, the big international institutions have set themselves the task of 'moralising' on land acquisition. They have drawn up codes of conduct, established guidelines, listed principles. But all of these rules are, by their very nature, non-binding. They are declarations of intent, which the individual investor or government can decide to follow or not as they see fit. 'They are nothing more than window dressing,' rages Henry.

In Saragih's opinion, the declarations of the big international organisations are eyewash. His analysis of the World Bank's role is merciless, his condemnation absolute: 'The institution is an integral part of this system. Its financial branch – The International Finance Corporation (IFC) – stimulates the agreements. It applies the necessary pressure on the governments who own the land to create a favourable environment for investment. And it often offers a guarantee – in the form of insurance – for investments that are considered less secure.'[9] The IFC has specifically leaned on various governments to get them to create more favourable conditions for investors by abolishing limits and by offering fiscal relief and various other concessions. Its experts have accompanied the investment agency teams to many different nations. In the meantime, another branch of the World Bank, the Multilateral Investment Guarantee Agency (MIGA), has busied itself offering guarantees for increased-risk investments. The model used is not a new one: the Bank has already used it in the past in the building or planning of large infrastructure projects, especially in Africa, such as the dams built in Lesotho and Uganda. The paradigm of reference is public-private partnership, where the construction of large projects or the management of goods which are already public – such as water, energy, land – are entrusted to private entities.[10]

This approach assumes that market forces cause development – and that the market must therefore be as free as possible from constrictions. 'Let's not be idiots about this. The World Bank mirrors the actions of the north against the people in the south,' emphasises Saragih. Here the peasant leader highlights a great contradiction: despite its name, the World Bank is the least representative of all the international institutions. Its headquarters is in Washington, and only a United States citizen can become its President. Decisions are made through voting, and yet each member is given more or less votes in proportion to the amount of funding it has put at the Bank's disposal. Instead of being a truly multilateral body, therefore, the World Bank often serves as a battering ram used by the wealthy countries to enact their policies in poorer ones.

Having promoted for years the so-called structural adjustment policies, through which governments in the south were pushed to privatise goods and services and open themselves up to the global market, the institution turned its focus to the implementation of 'poverty reduction strategies', with the Poverty Reduction Strategy Papers (PRSP) – policy documents in which international experts and the governments of the countries in question established the reforms required to reduce poverty. By involving civil society in the consultation process, the PRSP was supposed to represent a clean break with the past. The approach, however, is not much different, given that the World Bank places a series of conditions on every loan and every action. These conditions inevitably lead to solutions similar to those of the reviled structural adjustment plans, albeit in a less openly unilateral manner. While the mission of the World Bank is to reduce poverty, the ways in which that mission has been implemented have often been disastrous to say the least. It is also for this reason that Via Campesina and other farming associations are ferociously hostile to the organisation – and more generally to all the international institutions, which they see as being merely instruments of big business. 'The World Bank is part of this system that destroys our resources,' fumes Saragih. 'Even its presumed principles for responsible investment have been passed down from the powers above, drawn up without the involvement of the governments of poor countries or those people who suffer from these investments: the farmers, the indigenous population, the fishermen, the shepherds.'

A *masterpiece of acrobatics*

The bone of contention at this meeting of the Committee on World Food Security is precisely this. The big international institutions seem embarrassed: they support investments in agriculture in developing countries, but they cannot ignore the negative consequences these investments can produce in terms of access to land and water resources, the dislocation of communities, and the loss of biodiversity. This is because the large investments are primarily made to set up industrial plants for monocultures destined for exportation. The paradox, therefore, is that in many cases they end up further undermining the food sovereignty of the countries that have given away their land.

Caught up in these contradictions, the global organisations adopt a strategy of conditional approval, which often gives the impression that they are insisting that black is white. One prime example is the report drawn up by the World Bank on the subject, which is a masterpiece of acrobatics.[11] Published after lengthy talks and several press leaks, it is so contradictory that it has been interpreted in myriad different ways, some of them diametrically opposed. At the time of its release, some in the media claimed that 'The World Bank approves agricultural agreements', while others maintained that the Bank 'condemns them given that they put at risk small farmers' access to land'.[12] The journalists hadn't suddenly lost their minds: both of these affirmations appear in the text. On the one hand, the report argues that 'the large scales of the areas involved and their concentration in a relatively few nations with weak institutions render these investments dangerous'. On the other, it states that 'these dangers can be transformed into opportunities', given that investors could relaunch the development of agriculture in countries short of capital, and create greater productivity for small farmers.[13] Working on this premise, the World Bank drew up and announced certain principles for 'responsible investment in agriculture' (RAI), including the need not to undermine the food sovereignty of these nations, the stipulating of transparent agreements with the involvement of local communities, and the respecting of present rights regarding access to land, which are often customary rather than being legally defined on paper.[14] The RAI principles are a kind of joker that World Bank officials throw down to defend and give an air of continuity to their position: yes to investment, but in a responsible way. Develop, but for the common good. Produce on a large scale without interfering with access to land or water or with biodiversity. Principles which are all very appealing and laudable, but which in reality are not generally applied. As one uneasy World Bank official (who has worked for years on the issue of food security) tells me, strictly 'off the record' at the fringes of another international meeting: 'They are nice words. But the truth is that we provide the bread but nothing else to eat with it.'[15]

A dialogue among the deaf

On the third floor of the FAO building, one of the most crowded plenary sessions of the summit is underway. The theme is 'International Investment in Agriculture'. An enormous room hosts the delegates: there are respected ambassadors, several ministers for agriculture, FAO officials and members of farming organisations. The session begins with a number of brief presentations by representatives from the various United Nations agencies, the World Bank, and research centres. Some launch into PowerPoint presentations. Others read from pre-prepared speeches. Others still speak by rote.

Everybody has their say, and without giving much space to the previous speaker's comments. The representatives of FAO, IFAD and the World Bank present, with a few marginal differences, the positions of their respective organisations: investments are needed, but they must be made in a responsible fashion. All of them use the same kind of language that for the public institutions has become something of a *ritornello*: we must create the conditions so that this is a *win-win* situation.

'The public offices must identify priority areas to which they must attract agricultural investment, in order to reap the greatest possible benefits for the population,' says a senior FAO official. Then comes the representative from the Eastern Africa Farmers Federation who, in a vibrant tone, accuses 'governments who facilitate the hoarding of land by private entities. Because it is governments who create just the right conditions to enable private concerns to come and sack our land.' The governments in question who are present, such as that of Ethiopia, do not deign to respond. Then the floor is opened up to the public. The meeting itself follows the same structure. With what seems to be a meticulously planned alternating sequence, an institutional talk is followed by a civil society one, and so on. It's like watching a courteous duel, so courteous that the duellers don't even touch each other. Nobody cites anybody else. They hardly look each other in the eye. Everybody remains glued to their respective positions. The representatives of the farming organisations speak of the underselling of land; those from the institutions and governments of investments in agriculture. The former use terms such as 'theft', 'neo-colonialism', 'violated rights'. The latter, 'opportunity', 'development', 'productivity'. Two opposing models are coming face to face. One, supported by the big institutions, is banking on large private agencies, who they believe to be capable of relaunching large-scale production in an agricultural sector that is barely above subsistence level.

The other is that of the farming organisations, who demand respect for land rights and call for public investment.

These are not merely two different development models, but two different cultural models. The first imagines the earth as simply a place for producing on an industrial level in order to feed an ever-growing world population. The second defends the tradition of life in the fields, a relationship with the earth, farming expertise which has been passed down through the centuries, and rejects the idea of enormous monoculture plantations, which are only interested in exploiting the earth. The first has as its point of reference the urban world and city populations that are rocketing and need to be fed. The second is firmly rooted in the countryside. For those who believe in the first model, the others are a species of anachronistic savages, digging their heels in against modernity and defending a world that no longer exists. For the second group, the first are monsters to be resisted with all one's strength and with whom it's pointless to converse. The reference points of these two groups are not only diverse, they are antithetical, irreconcilable. The advocates of investment at whatever cost proudly cite the 'green revolution' that increased production out of all proportion in Asia in the 1960s and 1970s, due to the introduction of new technology (from the large-scale use of hybrid seeds to fertilisers and pesticides). The farming organisations respond that this revolution only brought large agribusiness groups into a position of enormous power, not to mention an unprecedented wave of suicides in rural India. The supporters of investment are strongly in favour of genetically modified organisms (GMO). For the farming representatives GMOs are a cancer infecting their fields.

A very special rapporteur

The very difficult role of mediator between these two incompatible positions has been given to a seemingly demure Belgian

Law Professor. Small in stature, with thinning hair, his expression framed by a pair of round glasses, Olivier De Schutter vaguely resembles Tintin. He certainly has the same physique as that intrepid globetrotting reporter, but also the same discretion and wit, a feigned absent-mindedness that permits him to put forward his arguments calmly but forcefully and to get his point across when all around him are shouting. UN Special Rapporteur on the Right to Food, De Schutter took on the role at the height of the food crisis in 2008. Catapulted onto the world stage at a time when all that was being talked about was price hikes and food riots, he displayed great competence and denounced at every opportunity what he saw as the main causes of the disaster: the development of biofuels and related financial speculation. As for land acquisitions, he has on several occasions expressed great reservations, so much so that he enjoys considerable respect among farming organisations. At the CFS summit it seems his presence is requested everywhere all at once. He is a strong advocate of dialogue and meetings, which means that here he is being worked off his feet. As I'm interviewing him in the hall of the FAO building, he is forced to interrupt our conversation twice when his collaborators implore him to hurry to a meeting in which speculation on food is being discussed. 'It's a very delicate meeting,' he offers apologetically as he flees, and later sends me a text asking me to email him with whatever further questions I need answered.

De Schutter is hardly ever in Lovanio, the small Belgian university town where he teaches International Law. More often than not he is travelling the world, on missions in the field or at evaluation meetings. His role is unique; his freedom of speech considerably greater than that of UN officials. His opinion is that of an independent expert who has been called to perform a particular function. He genuinely is a 'Special Rapporteur'. His predecessor, the Swiss deputy and essayist

Jean Ziegler, had made his mark with a number of particularly virulent statements, such as when he likened agrofuels to 'weapons of mass destruction'. De Schutter's style is decidedly more sober. He doesn't uses phrases for effect, but this doesn't make him any less incisive. With a more academic approach, he criticises the way in which the problem of hunger and malnutrition is dealt with by the other UN bodies: 'Hunger is often considered by international agencies to be a production or availability problem – this is why FAO encourages an increase in production while the World Food Programme distributes food wherever there is a particular need due to famine, a bad harvest or other crisis situations. I believe, on the other hand, that the principal causes of hunger are discrimination and marginalisation, together with the fact that governments don't pay enough heed to the needs of their people, and adopt policies that can increase hunger instead of alleviating it.' One of these policies, De Schutter openly declares, is the indiscriminate renting of land to international investors who have precious little interest in the food security of the countries in which they invest. Over the course of our intermittent interview, he sketches for me a comprehensive, up-to-date and detailed picture of the situation, highlighting the many contradictions that litter the debate. 'According to FAO estimates, there are 400 million hectares of available land, of which 202 million can be found in sub-Saharan Africa. The problem is that what is considered "available land" is land with less than twenty-five people per square kilometre. This land is often being used by small farmers of nomadic livestock who do not have the deeds for the land that they are depending on for their survival, and thus have no legal recourse against their eviction. This "available land" concept is one that is easy to manipulate.' 'So in actual fact what is being assigned is used land?' 'Each context must be studied case-by-case. In general, I think it's necessary to underline that we are facing a highly paradoxical situation. On the one hand there is a continuous demographic rise and in rural areas farmers are cultivating plots that are constantly getting smaller, on the other we are told that there are 200 million hectares of available land. If all this available land really exists, the first priority is to decide who it should be given to. But this question has become taboo, precisely because of large-scale investment. Instead of distributing the land to small farmers by virtue of adequate agrarian reform and a system of loans that can increase their productivity, it is offered instead to big investors. These investors put at risk not only access to land but also access to water. And they turn small farmers into either day labourers or migrants who are destined to swell the lines of the urban poor.' Given this approach, it's not surprising that De Schutter is extremely critical of the RAI principles promoted by the World Bank. 'These principles assume that every government only has two options to choose from: to welcome an investor or not to welcome him. In actual fact, the real question, the real choice is: should we invest in small family farming, distributing land, building infrastructure, supplying storing facilities, or should we bank on large plantations? This question is crucial, but it is avoided, because it would imply agrarian reform and deny the governments the advantage, immediate in the short term but potentially counterproductive in the long term, which comes from opening the market to the big investors.'

De Schutter has compiled his own list of principles which he has submitted to the UN Human Rights Council.[16] His list is very different to that of the World Bank. He doesn't start from the premise that large-scale investments in agriculture are necessarily a good thing. In fact, he lays down a series of very stringent conditions: the land mustn't be ceded without the consent of the community present on the territory, the investments must benefit the local population, they must create employment, and they mustn't impede access to land or the food sovereignty of the states in question. A percentage of the produce must be sold at local market level, and this percentage must be able to increase in a proportion agreed in advance if the price of food produce on the international market exceeds a certain level.

De Schutter is fighting to promote a particular idea of rural development which doesn't have as its only point of reference the large monocultures or industrial plantations. He submits his reports to the General Assembly of the United Nations, he assists at every summit on food security, and he advises governments and officials. But his list is only a declaration of intent, which doesn't constrain anybody or anything. In a moment of great lucidity, from the conference table of FAO's plenary session on international investments, the Special Rapporteur reveals what would seem to be the intrinsic weakness of the entire summit: 'Here we have the governments, the farming organisations, the international institutions. Are there, by any chance, any representatives from the private sector in the room? If there are any private investors here, please raise your hands.' No hands are raised. Silence pervades the room. Those who have decided to invest in land are elsewhere.

The path that links Wall Street to the farm

I get to meet some of these private investors barely a month later in Geneva, at a glittering conference entitled 'Global AgInvesting Europe'. Soyatech, an American agency specialising in the supply of information and communication services to the food industry, and HighQuest Partners, a consulting firm, have organised this two-day convention reserved for businessmen, dealers from the industry, and managers of financial holdings interested in getting into the agricultural sector. It's a highly exclusive event: an entrance ticket for the two days costs $1,995, reduced to $995 for those from non-profit institutions.

LAND GRABBING

After protracted negotiations with Soyatech's communications manager – including telephone calls, emails, the sending of old articles of mine and my curriculum vitae, and satisfactory assurances of my character and professionalism – I manage to get my hands on a press pass. This allows me to attend the meeting for free, along with all the collateral events – cocktails, lunches, dinners, and so on. At an early hour on the morning of the first day I go down to the Intercontinental, the luxury hotel on the outskirts of the city where the event is being hosted. The instructional email had advised those attending to dress *business casual*, a formula that struck me as a little contradictory. Not exactly proficient in the finer points of the American dress-code system, I decide to err on the side of business rather than casual: I don an elegant white shirt, a black light wool suit and a tie. As soon as I arrive, I realise that *business casual* in American basically means 'wear whatever you want'. Some are wearing ties, some are sporting dickey bows. Others have opted for a simple shirt. There's even one man in shorts, a long-sleeved top and a pair of gym shoes. My look happens to be the most popular, which gives me hope that I'll be able to blend in. It doesn't take long before this particular hope is dashed: everybody around me has a gigantic plastic rectangle around their necks, making them instantly identifiable. I make my way to the reception point and get my own personal badge. In a very American way, my first name is written, incorrectly, and in large letters – Stephano. Underneath, in smaller print, my surname and my function. I soon learn that the colour of the badge is a discriminating factor: blue is for the speakers, green for the sponsors, purple for those who have paid for their tickets, black for the organisers, red – the one I and a handful of other colleagues are wearing – for the press. The badge is important. You must wear it at all times, because it defines who you are. Before anyone says a word to you, they

94

all look at your badge, to find out who they are dealing with and how much of their time you are worth if there's going to be a conversation. And here, everybody talks with everybody. These two days are a networking event, set up especially for meeting people. There's no hint of shyness or reluctance. The participants have come here to listen to the speeches of course, but mostly they've come to make contacts, create business rapports, form mutually convenient relations. Everyone greets each other with hearty handshakes which are quickly and automatically accompanied by an exchange of business cards. The participants give off the impression of belonging to a closed circuit, and they behave like companions setting off on the same adventure. The badges around their necks are a sign of their belonging to a group, a viaticum for starting a conversation with the stranger beside you – because he's not really a stranger, but a member of your community that you just haven't happened to meet yet.

I enter the conference room. It's full – about three hundred people in total. On the screen at the far end of the room the meeting's symbol stands out: an open field that's just been harvested, in which a shock of wheat has been replaced by a rolled stack of hundred dollar bills. The message is clear and direct: this conference will help you to transform agricultural products into ready cash. The ambience is extremely convivial. In the space of ten minutes I've already met everyone around me: there's the American, Drew, who works for a hedge fund based in New York, but who's been living in Ireland for the past few years. He's come – so he tells me without going into detail – 'to get information for a deal I want to set up in the next few months'. There's Carlos the Brazilian, who has an investment fund back home and is here, among other things, 'to look for partners'. There's the Frenchman Pierre, the manager of a finance group from the United Arab

Emirates that 'hasn't invested in land yet. And that's why I'm here.' At the end of the room, somewhat detached from the others, there's a group of Russian businessmen. Two distinctive clues give away their nationality: the high alcohol intake, even although it's early in the morning, and a trail of women, who have come with them to translate everything that is said. It's not just the language barrier that explains the Russians' lack of openness. They prefer to keep themselves to themselves, registering the information they need, and perhaps participating at a few selected meetings.

The organisers of the event welcome everyone with a brief introduction. A small, bald man with a feeble voice takes the floor, and smiles a little artificially as he apologises to 'our European friends, because in a typically American fashion we're starting our work at 8.30 in the morning'. Hunt Stookey, manager of HighQuest Partners, outlines in two minutes what is going to be discussed for the next forty-eight hours: 'Dear friends and colleagues, welcome to Geneva and to the first AgInvesting conference to be held in Europe. We're delighted to see such a high degree of participation in our first conference outside of North America. After two years out of the headlines, food and agriculture is back in the news. The effects of the bad Russian grain harvest have combined with those of a corn harvest in the United States which was disappointing to say the least. For those of us who work every day in the sector, this was no great surprise. We were expecting it, it was only a question of when, not if. The global market of basic food produce is going to have to face a shortage in the near future. The demographic rise, the demand for animal proteins (and also for feed) in the developing world, and biofuels are together producing an inexorable increase in demand. All it takes is one bad harvest to bring on a global crisis. For all these reasons, the agriculture sector is an extremely promising sector for your investments. If recent trends continue, and we are certain that they will, we can say that land is destined in the coming years to attract tens if not hundreds of billions of dollars. Our programme will help you to understand what your best options are, thanks to the guidance of people who have already invested in the sector, fund managers, and renowned managers and academics who have been studying the tendencies of the agricultural market for years.'

The programme is to include many different kinds of talks. University professors will explain why the world is on the brink of collapse due to hunger, and why land is the new good to invest in. Investment fund managers will extol the monumental returns open to their subscribers. There will be a detailed analysis of the pros and cons of investment in land in various regions of the world: the risks by country, the regimes of ownership, the costs of labour. The scene seems a little surreal. The speakers are almost all former Wall Street sharks, golden boys and girls previously employed by the likes of Goldman Sachs or Morgan Stanley, who have now ventured out on their own to try their hand in the agricultural investment sector. They are financiers dissecting the productivity of harvests, tilling and sowing methods, irrigation systems. As one manager of a big American hedge fund puts it, 'we want to close the gap between Wall Street and the path that leads to the farm, because you can't grow grain on Wall Street, and you can't grow it in the City of London either'. In order to make the concept even clearer, he gives a PowerPoint presentation in which first we see the trading floor at the New York Stock Exchange, then a farm somewhere in the world, and finally a dirt road supposed to link these two universes which have been so far apart until now. 'Whoever sets off on this path is going to reap the benefits of a great challenge and a remarkable yield,' the manager assures us to the applause of the crowd, before their thoughts turn to the scheduled coffee break.

Water is the new frontier

In the meantime, a handful of protesters have gathered outside the hotel to protest against the planet's 'hunger merchants'. It's a terribly Swiss affair: the participants form an orderly line on the pavement, almost in single file. They speak through a loudspeaker one at a time, following a pre-arranged order. The police have cordoned off the entrance to the hotel, even though there's really no need. The protestors are anything but bellicose. One of the Soyatech managers watches them as he smokes a cigarette outside. He's looks on with a mix of distaste and compassion. Then he comes up to me, and checks out my badge. 'You a journalist? What do you think of this protest?' 'I don't know. Who are they?' I lie, having seen the call-to-arms, or rather sit-in, on the net. 'They're those guys from Farmlandgrab, that activist website that's always attacking us. They call us "hoarders of land", "lackeys of capitalism", but they don't get it that they're the ones against progress. They say we steal people's land. What we really do is bring technology, invest in sectors nobody invests in, increase productivity. They don't understand this. They want everything to remain the way it is, with people dying of hunger.' The rhetoric of the *win-win situation* rings out like a mantra at this Geneva meeting too. If there's one thing the managers gathered here want to avoid like the plague, it's newspaper headlines accusing them of speculating on poverty. This is why they argue that their investments are vital 'to feed the world'. This is why they always speak – often after listing in detail the double-figure profits available – of 'social and environmental responsibility'. And this is why they've organised a panel with the title 'How Can we Invest Responsibly in Agriculture?' to which they've invited a number of academics who are critical of the present trend of sprawling investments in agriculture. 'It's no coincidence they've put this at the end,' says Drew beside me. 'They had to do it. But the truth is that all the participants, including myself, are only here for one reason: to find out how to make easy money.'

And to make easy money, you have to bet on the scarcity of food, and worm your way into the fallacies of the system. In mid-afternoon, our friend Stookey climbs onto the stage to announce the estimates on the American corn harvest, which have just been released by the Department of Agriculture. 'Dear friends and colleagues, the harvest this year is going to be poor,' he says with a satisfied look, to a hearty round of applause. This bad harvest will increase the price of corn and, in a domino effect, also those of all the other food commodities, which will generate profits for the various groups present in the room. These investors, who insist they want to feed the world, are delighted at the lack of food, because a lack of food is going to make them more money.

The speeches continue. The possibilities for investment in agriculture in various parts of the world are analysed: from South America to Eastern Europe, from Russia to Africa. Detailed explanations are given of the various investment possibilities in the entire productive chain: from direct participation in the exploitation of land, to investment in a division company, to a simple one in commodities. A list is proposed of countries in which it is easy and relatively safe to invest, and another of states where the risk is higher (this latter includes states whose governments have socialist tendencies, such as Venezuela, Bolivia and Ecuador). Then a man in his early fifties takes the stage, sporting a blue jacket, striped shirt, thick grey hair and a sly look. He starts his presentation with an affirmation delivered in a solemn tone: 'Water is the new frontier.' Judson Hill is the Executive Director of NGP-Global Adaptation Partners, an investment group that in recent years has bet practically everything on the blue gold.[17] 'Water is going to get scarcer and scarcer. Agricultural development is going to require it more and more: people should be investing in this sector.' Hill nevertheless goes on to acknowledge the many difficulties any investor may face: water is a *local commodity*, in that it's difficult to transport, and it has 'a very strong emotive value for communities'.

Someone in the audience raises his hand: 'Explain to us then how we can make money with water!' 'Water is a public good in many parts of the world,' continues Hill. 'But the tendency is towards privatisation. Whoever succeeds in controlling the water reserves, by intercepting the tendencies of states to delegate services and distribution to private companies, is going to make a mountain of cash.'

Land-grabbing pensioners

In the past five years, tens of billions of dollars have been moved from the purely financial sector into agriculture, both in the commodity market (grain, corn, rice, soya) and through direct participation in various types of investment funds linked to agricultural production. Many players have joined the rush for the green gold: big financiers such as Lord Jacob Rothschild,[18] traditional agribusiness conglomerates like Cargill and Louis Dreyfuss,[19] investment banks, and even pension funds from wealthy nations, anxious to offer the necessary security to their subscribers. This means that, perhaps unbeknownst to them, ex-labourers and ex-farmers are also implicated, through the investment of their pension funds in land grabbing.

Pension funds do not invest directly, but place their capital in funds created *ad hoc* by companies which serve either as intermediaries or direct operators in the sector. Based on certain islands in the Caribbean or in the English Channel, where fiscal legislation is anything but rigorous, these companies invest in land all over the world. The instruments they use to do so are varied.[20] There are *hedge funds* – speculative funds that operate without leverage limits or, in other words, no barriers to short buying with respect to real available finance. There are *private equity funds* – funds not quoted on the stock market that are geared towards private subjects, and that deal in medium-term investments (three or four years) before selling off and pocketing the profits. Then there are the more classic *mutual funds* – shared investment funds where small savers put together capital which can then be invested in the stock market or used to buy company shares.

The money invested is destined to grow exponentially. This explains why the conference room in the Hotel Intercontinental is so crowded and why there are quite a few pension fund representatives who have paid two thousand dollars for the pleasure of being here. 'We decided to organise these events due to the urging of various institutional organisations who came to us looking for advice,' Stookey makes a point of stressing. A number of these intermediary companies that have entered into the agriculture business have the support of large institutions such as the World Bank. This is true of Altima Partners, which set up an agriculture fund – registered in the Cayman Islands – with the direct collaboration of the International Finance Corporation (IFC) of the World Bank. The institution's private branch invested seventy-five million dollars in the project, or approximately 12 percent of the fund's entire capital.[21] This is also the case for the London firm, Chayton Capital, which invests in agriculture in Zambia. From the stage in Geneva, the firm's Director and founder, Neil Crowder, who spent many years at Goldman Sachs before going out on his own, proudly talks about a contract he signed directly with Zambia and with the World Bank. When I approach him after his speech to learn more, he tells me that the Bank participates through MIGA, its insurance branch, to 'partly cover the political risks of the investment'.

Neil is the spitting image of an English Lord: elegant, affable, most accommodating. He certainly has a different way about him compared to most of the other participants: unlike the Americans, who are more direct and take your badge in their hands as soon as you approach them, Neil simply casts a discreet glance at it. He answers every question in a very measured way, choosing each word carefully, even though ours is an informal chat at a table during a coffee break. His eyes move in quick spurts, which creates a certain dissonance with the slowness of his speech. As we talk, I get the distinct feeling that he's trying to size me up without letting on that he's doing so. Then again, it may simply be a case of the notorious English sangfroid, which stands out here considering that it differs so much from the more convivial general tone of the meeting. Neil is cordial but distant, friendly but never expansive. When I ask him what his objectives are, he defines himself as a 'not particularly aggressive investor', and admits that the World Bank's support was decisive in convincing his group to invest in Zambia. 'I'm not at all sure that I would have entered into this deal without this kind of security. We nevertheless envisage good returns in the medium term,' he states, without revealing too much.[22]

The three p's: profit, planet, people

Someone who has no qualms about promising astronomical profits, however, is Susan Payne, Director and founder of Emergent Asset Management, another company with its headquarters in London, and which has invested, through various private equity funds, in the acquisition and exploitation of land in five southern African countries, with plans to expand even further.[23] Susan is magnetic. Not very tall, about fifty years old, copper-red hair, she has a look that captures you, envelops you, compels you to listen to her. As soon as she begins her speech, silence pervades the conference room. Everybody stares at her: the pens that have been doodling, like that of the man sitting beside me, come to a brisk halt. Cell phones on which others have been happily texting are put away. Even the Russians at the end of the room start listening attentively to their interpreters. Payne describes her job and defines investment in land as 'one of the most exciting investment opportunities in Africa'. She talks of returns of 25 percent because, as she underlines in her strong, precise and vaguely stentorian voice, 'Africa is the new frontier. Land is cheap and, with the right investments in technology, it's entirely possible to increase productivity, earn a lot of money and benefit the local population.' As she shows pictures of the industrial farms that her group has created in Zambia, she reels off both figures and certainties: '60 percent of the world's uncultivated land is in Africa. Africa is destined to grow. And we must take part in this growth.'

Susan considers herself a pioneer. She's fully convinced of her mission, and fully aware of how extremely convincing she can be. 'In the twenty-four years that I've been working in finance, this is the most exciting, useful and enthralling thing I've ever done', she tells me as I and a colleague from Austrian Radio, Christian Brueser, talk with her in a little room reserved for the press. This woman likes to talk about what she does. Our conversation – which started with a 'not more than ten minutes, because I'd like to hear the other speeches' – lasts almost an hour. On and on she flows, like a waterfall: she describes her many trips to Zambia, her encounters with the managers and people in the area, the expeditions she organises for investors interested in her fund ('who need to understand, to actually touch the product they are investing in'). She talks of economies of scale, of integrated systems, of technology to be imported. She repeatedly uses the *win-win situation* formula. She feels compelled by a higher mission: to bring about a green revolution through investments which will increase the productivity of the fields and replenish the countries in which she invests. She strongly believes in what she does: in addition to her role as finance manager she takes part in various microcredit projects focusing on Africa, and is one of the founders of an NGO seeking to advance medical knowledge in the continent with the help of multi-media tools. Hers are not empty words. She seems genuinely moved when she talks about the places in which she invests. 'It's not easy going to places that are extremely poor. It's hard to understand the level of poverty if you don't actually see it with your own eyes.' I remind her that it's precisely that poverty that allows her to obtain land at dirt-cheap prices. 'The land is cheap, but our agreements aren't unfair. In Zambia we pay between 800 and 1,000 dollars a hectare, compared to the 5,000 we'd pay in Argentina or the 24,000 we'd pay in Germany. We don't pay much, but we pay enough. And we also invest, create employment, increase food security wherever we operate.' Susan is unshakable. She never shows the slightest sign of irritation, not even at the most provocative of questions. She responds point-for-point as she looks you straight in the eye, like a hunter eyeing his prey through the sights of his rifle.

The strong point of her discussion, and one that she repeats over and over, is this: Emergent Asset Management's agricultural fund is not only a financial tool. It follows the line from start to finish. It selects the land, works out the agreements with the governments, organises the harvests. 'We have set up an integrated system. We are directly active in the business.' Eighty-five percent of the produce from its farms is destined for the internal market: which protects the company from accusations of direct divestment of resources. Relations with the governments are excellent, she assures me. When she tells me about 9,000 hectares she has obtained in Zimbabwe (one of the least promising places to do business if you are white, not to mention British, given that since 2000 Robert Mugabe has tended to dispossess white colonies), she candidly replies that she has 'a very able manager on the ground who has excellent links with the government'.

A former Director at Goldman Sachs International, Susan Payne is a champion of responsible investment, and was co-opted by the World Bank into the group that drew up the famous RAI principles. Returning momentarily to the pragmatism of a financial operator, she stresses that responsible investment is desirable not only from a moral viewpoint, but also from an economic one: 'It's not possible to work in a hostile environment. Sooner or later people are going to revolt against you.' Her philosophy can be summarised by the three p's: *profit*, *planet* and *people*. Make a profit, do good to the planet, be on the side of the people. So she tries to convince whoever she's talking to that these three things are not contradictory – that it's possible to obtain enormous returns while minding the environment and assisting local populations.

Susan seems sincere. When she speaks, her big brown eyes light up. Her speech is peppered with references to the future, her rhetoric awash with affirmations such as 'our adventure', 'a new frontier', 'the great open field in front of us'. She probably feels like a twenty-first-century cowgirl exploring virgin territories rich with opportunities. There is one difference, however, between her and those pioneers of the nineteenth century Wild West: she knows that the eyes of the world are on her and fellow adventurers. She knows that the land may be virgin, but it's not uninhabited. And she is aware that in order to carry off a project of this kind today, she must give the impression of absolute transparency. She therefore answers, without a trace of reticence, all questions on her work's impact on the territories, on possible negative fallouts, on doubts put forward by NGOs with respect to this new wave of investment in agriculture. 'Things should be examined case-by-case. We produce mostly for the internal market and we pay great attention to the company's social responsibility.' I ask her what she thinks about those companies that buy up land at a dollar a hectare and produce only for exportation. She answers that she can only speak for what her group does, not for others. And then she invites me to go and visit the farms in southern Africa that are directly run by her group. 'You will see with your own eyes what we have set up', she says with a smile at the end of our conversation, before shaking my hand and returning to the conference room.

'Let's hope we don't get sent packing'

Susan Payne is the quintessential finance manager who throws herself into the new agribusiness sector. Modern, convincing and, most of all, inspired by good intentions. Many of the other participants at the conference use her very same words. The most widespread formula used in the room is: 'We are not an NGO, but we want to contribute to the future of the planet.' Everybody professes that their objective is the general wellbeing of people, along with the good health of their pockets. As the speeches roll on, I find myself a little wrong-footed: I'd expected to meet avid financiers who couldn't care less about the environment, were indifferent to the plight of landless farmers, and insensitive to the poverty of families who can't put two daily meals together. Instead, I'm at a meeting where every time money is mentioned it is immediately qualified by phrases such as 'a better world', 'social responsibility', 'food sovereignty', and so on. Everything seems designed to be politically and ecologically correct: the Media Director has sent the other accredited journalists and me an email with the biographies of the participants, and the specification that 'this material won't appear in the press kit for the good of the environment'.

This gloss of good intentions is sullied only at brief moments of epiphany, during impromptu and informal discussions in corridors away from the speeches. Like the one I have with Mikael Von Euw from Zurich, who I meet at a cocktail party organised for the end of the first day. Surrounded by little tables laid with shrimp and salmon hors d'oeuvres and other titbits, this stocky thirty-five-year-old sits apart from the others, drinking a beer. I approach him and we introduce ourselves. He tells me he's the manager of a 'family office', which really means that he and his brother look after the fund of a wealthy family. 'We've put a lot of that money into a company in Mozambique. We'll be producing some stuff for the local market, but mostly we'll be concentrating on biofuels. We've signed a leasing agreement for twenty-five years.' Mikael claims to have obtained the land for a symbolic rent, which he doesn't want to specify, limiting himself to adding 'really symbolic'. As we crunch on prawn crackers and down some excellent white wine, he tells me about the feasibility studies he carried out together with a South African partner, describing the technology they had to bring in, and giving a few details on their interaction with the Maputo government. 'They gave us fiscal exemption, they did absolutely everything to pave our way.' By the time the fourth glass has gone down, Mikael is a lot less reticent. He tells me about a trip he made to the region, 'florid and luxurious, like a paradise on earth'. He digresses for a moment to talk about the 'extraordinary beauty of the local women'. Then he looks me in the eye and says: 'It was all so fast, maybe too fast. To be honest, I don't understand what they get out of this. I sincerely hope that there isn't some trick, and that once the investment is made they don't send us packing.' Then he smiles, gulps down another prawn and says – as I continue drinking even though my head is starting to spin – 'So far, so good. Business is risk too. Let's hope we don't get sent packing.'

The losers in a win-win situation

Mikael's words have given me a reading of the intentions of the participants, of the sentiments common to those who have signed up to this meeting. But they don't supply me with an adequate or complete response to the apparent contradiction I've been asking myself about for the entire duration of the conference. Namely: how is it possible to argue that you can make a pile of money, without anyone having to pay the price? How is it possible that in this agrarian version of Monopoly everybody's a winner, and there are no losers? How is it possible to make a 25 percent annual profit, produce for the local market, and create employment, without someone having to cough up something? The unanimity of the speakers has almost got me on board; the repeated expressions of good intentions don't seem to me to be just a simple exercise in hypocrisy. Here everyone wants to make money, but they want to do so without creating imbalances or stamping on anybody's rights. Mikael, who questions the real benefits for the Mozambique government, says he is 'worried about the working conditions of the locals', to whom he offers 'above-average salaries, and also healthcare'. Even when his alcohol intake passes the point at which he lets down his guard, he still talks about development as well as profit. I don't get the impression that I'm sitting in a den of unscrupulous neo-colonialists as they divide up the good land of the southern hemisphere.

Of course, the truth is that the big land grabbers aren't here. Geneva has basically attracted relatively small groups that have taken over a few thousand hectares each. There's no sign of the big Indian or South Korean multinationals that have invested in Ethiopia and Madagascar, or the managers of the sovereign funds from the Arab nations who rent land at 100,000 hectares a turn. What we have here are small and medium-sized investors, talking about their experiences and promoting their products to an audience of their peers: small and medium-sized groups that are thinking about investing in agriculture or have done so on a smaller scale.

Nevertheless, having thought about my sense of displacement, I realise that the fulcrum of the question lies elsewhere. Here there are no capitalist vultures who steal the land and chase away the farmers with their rifles. The investors are well-meaning people, almost all of whom genuinely believe that their money initiates a virtuous circle, or a game in which everyone will come out a winner. The terms of the question are different: nobody wants to impose himself on anybody else. It's simply a matter of a collision between different concepts of territory and development. Even the small and medium-sized groups have a precise model in mind, which is the same one so clearly analysed by Henry Saragih at the FAO summit: the model of large-scale cultivation, in which agriculture aims at maximum production by exploiting the land as much as possible; the model promoted by the World Bank and by the large international organisations. This model and that of the small farmers who produce on a smaller scale are simply not compatible. They are opposites, from both a practical and an ontological point of view. This is the real contradiction that enlivened both the meeting in Geneva and the one at FAO, and that runs through the whole of the present debate on land grabbing. The dilemma – small agriculture versus industrial farms – tears to shreds the principles of responsible investment, rendering them pointless. It defines the real crux of the discussion, offering a choice that is cruel but clear: it's either us or them. This is pointed out in a lucid speech given by a fund manager who invests in South America: 'There's no point trying to fool ourselves. Large-scale agricultural businesses take land, water and markets from small farmers. We're going to sell our products at a lower price and we're going to compete with small family farmers. Choices have to be made, political ones too: I believe that what the world needs most is an agricultural sector that is productive and large-scale. But it's not possible to carry through with this model without someone having to pay the price.' The political choices are being made, and they favour investments by large private groups while leaving small agricultural producers behind, a fact that Olivier De Schutter denounces at every possible opportunity. Having understood this, I can position the meeting in Geneva better within the broader scheme of things. It's another episode in the great global shift in the agricultural equilibrium. Viewed from a long-term perspective, it is a repetition of the traditional conflict between the city and the country: the urban populace, including its poor, are generally in favour of large investments, because they can lower the prices of agricultural produce at local markets and thus increase their spending power. But the corollary of this short-term beneficial effect can be devastating for everybody, because the farmers dispossessed by this policy will throng to the cities, offering low-cost labour and competing for jobs with the existing urban poor.

Something other than a *win-win situation*, the 'green revolution' proposed for Africa and elsewhere creates a long list of losers who have not been fully taken into consideration, not only by the investors at the Hotel Intercontinental who are basically just doing their job, but also in the rooms of those big international organisations whose official mandate is 'the reduction of poverty'.

CHAPTER 4

Chicago: The Hunger Market

The external walls are white, smooth and squared. The entrance is a revolving door that leads into a semi-lit cavern. The dark corridors are rendered even duller by lighting that feigns warmth but creates an unnatural effect. Imposing and majestic, tall enough to have held the record as the tallest building in the city for many years, the Chicago Board of Trade skyscraper has the look of an impregnable fortress. No sign appears to alert passers by to its presence, despite rising at the centre of the Loop, the city's busy business district. No symbol of American self-celebration like the enormous stars and stripes that hang at the entrance to the New York Stock Exchange on Wall Street. Even the statue of Cerere, the goddess of agriculture who stands on top of the skyscraper, is without a face. Almost as if to say: beyond the stock exchange there's nothing to see. The building seems to stand on its own: as if whoever built it wished to avoid all contamination with the external world, to exemplify the secretive and almost esoteric nature of the dealings that go on inside it.

And yet, together with the skyline that extends along the banks of the gigantic Lake Michigan, this austere monolith is the most concrete symbol of this white and attractive city, the home of gangsters and adventurers, merchants and fraudsters. The history of this stock market encapsulates that of the city and, in part, of the entire United States of America. Founded in 1848, when Chicago was still an agglomerate of shacks stacked on top of each other on the banks of the lake, it left its mark throughout the various stages by which the *windy city* became the capital of the Midwest. It was the time of the open frontier, of development towards the West. Of an America which, on the eve of the War of Secession, was seeking to invent itself as a nation. But also the time of commercial capitalism, advancing on tracks and along rivers, transporting merchandise and men, moulding the character of a future country.

Eighteen-forty-eight is a key year for Chicago: it sees the opening of the canal that links the Illinois river, a tributary of the Mississippi, with Lake Michigan, itself linked by Lake Erie and the Erie canal to New York and the Atlantic coast. This same crucial year also sees the inauguration of the first railway line, the Galena and Chicago Union. Barely ten miles long, just twelve years later it will have stretched to six thousand miles. Chicago establishes itself as a strategic centre, a junction for the river and rail throughways which link the great prairies of the interior with the urban centres of the East Coast.[1]

Thus in no time at all this small Illinois town grows beyond all proportion to become the main exchange centre for the cereals and meat produced in the prairies of the West. Corn flows in from Iowa, grain from Kansas and Nebraska, cattle from Wisconsin. Seeing the city inundated with tons of agricultural produce, overrun by swarms of small farmers and crammed with herds of animals destined for slaughter, a group of businessmen realise which way the wind is blowing. They meet up in a basement, and found a trading centre which would become the Chicago Board of Trade. The founders – not all agricultural traders: there's a librarian, a pharmacist, a grocer, a leather worker and various other types – understand that the market is too unstable: in winter prices shoot through the roof, whereas at harvest time farmers are selling below cost to get rid of their surplus. Some farmers, not at all convinced by the cost of storage compared to the selling price, end up pouring their excess grain and corn into the lake. The stock market is founded as an attempt to correct this mechanism. By creating a neutral meeting point for those buying and those selling, they invent a concept that will catch on like wildfire: 'futures', or contracts on future values. The basis of this mechanism is that the buyer and the seller sign an agreement for a delivery at a future date. They are there-fore betting on the product's value at the time of delivery: a bet that guarantees that the producer will be able to sell at that date for a determined price, and that the buyer will be able to purchase on that date at a specific cost. In other words, it allows people to plan their investments, thereby offering what is technically referred to as hedging. Hedging consists in assuming a position on the futures market which is the oppo-site of the position one holds in the real economy. The agri-cultural producer – of grain or corn, for example – at the moment of sowing undertakes to buy a number of grain and corn futures with delivery six months from the present time. He is buying virtual grain and corn at a determined price. If the harvest is a bad one, his futures will increase in value, and he will be able to compensate for the loss on the ground with the earnings accrued, i.e. the difference between the price he paid to buy the futures and the value that these have now reached. Vice versa, if the harvest is a good one and the futures have consequently fallen in value, he will have losses on the stock market but will gain from the increased value of his actual produce. The same principles, although in reverse, apply for the buyers – those market operators working in the sector that transform agricultural products. They place futures on the market, which means they sell virtual-products that they wish to buy at a future date. If the harvest is bad, they will pay more for the produce than they actually need to, but their increased spending will be compensated by a rise in the value of their futures. If, on the other hand, the harvest is good, they will lose on the financial market but pay less for the real produce.

But it isn't just the farmers and the buyers that deal in futures. From their very inception, various other players start attending the trading centre, transforming it into a kind of big casino. As a prediction about what will happen, the future contract is by its very nature a kind of wager. And a form of speculation. Given that future shares can be sold before the expiry of their contract, the Chicago stock market increasingly becomes a battlefield for gamblers, some more hardened than others. There is one substantial difference with respect to the casino, however: the combinations of red and black on a roulette table are uniquely determined by the laws of probability, whereas the value of futures on the raw material market is linked, at least initially, to a real and tangible good. Whoever predicts a bad harvest is stimulated to buy, because he believes that in the future the prices will rise and he will be able to sell his contract at a higher price. Whoever believes the harvest will be good is tempted to sell to compensate for a fall in the contract value. But the link with the real economy is not always as precise as this, because if everybody sells, prices will drop. If everybody buys – or if a few individuals buy everything – the prices will rocket. Put another way, betting on futures of a particular good can change its value, especially if individuals with significant financial clout throw their hat into the ring. Many times over the years some big speculator has tried to monopolise the market of a particular agricultural product at the Chicago stock market, by buying tonnes of futures in order to drive the price sky high and then, having control of the market, selling at exorbitant prices for great personal gain.

This was tried as far back as 1897 by a certain Joseph Leiter, a twenty-eight-year-old loose cannon who used his father's fortune to bloat the price of grain in one year from 67 cents to \$1.85 a bushel,[2] before failing miserably and losing a million dollars – a colossal sum at the time.[3] The mechanism, from which derives the term *to corner the market*, is prohibited in theory but is difficult to identify. Throughout the history of the Chicago Board of Trade, many attempts have been made to corner the market. Some have been successful. Others, like that of Leiter, have failed, leading to astronomical losses for the wild gamblers involved. The most famous case in Italy was that of Raul Gardini's Ferruzzi group who in 1989 bought future contracts for thirty-three million bushels of soya, approximately twice the amount available to those who had placed the futures on the market, such as big American agribusiness companies like Bunge, Continental and Cargill. The only way these companies could honour such a commitment would have been to buy the soya from Ferruzzi, generating immense profits for the Gardini company. But the board of the Chicago stock market blocked the operation and imposed an immediate liquidation of the contracts for 'distorting the market', which led to losses for Ferruzzi of 435 billion lire. Gardini consistently denied any intention to speculate and claimed that it needed that quantity of soya for the group's factories, which were contracted to supply feed to China and Russia. Whether or not the intentions of the Ferruzzi group were predatory, the soya war of 1989 – along with other cornering episodes that have occurred since the stock market's inception – clearly show how the future shares market, created to bring stability, has often had the opposite effect.

In this game of bet-raising, the Chicago Board of Trade – absorbed in 2007 into the Chicago Mercantile exchange, which deals in fixed-term interest rates, share indexes, currency and goods exchange – has established itself globally as the venue *par excellence* for future shares. As its own website points out, 'we supply a greater range of future products and options than any other stock market, covering all of the most important sectors'.⁴ Today, the Chicago trading floor plays host to the exchange of more than ten million contracts a day.⁵ It began with futures on agricultural products, and has grown to include futures on petrol products, on government bonds from the US Treasury, and on so-called options, a sort of insurance for the future, or futures on futures, in a virtually endless game of arithmetic squares where the link with the real economy becomes increasingly tenuous, and the outcome of negotiations increasingly related to the traders' mood swings or speculative tricks as opposed to objective evaluations.

This explains why, in 2007 and 2008, when the prices of food goods start to rise and protests break out in many parts of the world, the spotlight is fixed on the discreet skyscraper on Jackson Boulevard. The Chicago stock market is seen as the main culprit for the crime. Its speculators are identified as being responsible for the criminal increase in prices, and swarms of journalists gather from the four corners of the globe to try to find out who exactly it is that's starving the planet.

The ring of tarantula victims

I'm one of these journalists looking for a scoop. After weeks of exasperating emails to and fro with the stock market's communications office, I get authorisation to enter the building, film the trading and have some expert traders explain to me the mechanisms behind fluctuations in prices and futures on primary food produce. Having jumped through several bureaucratic hoops, such as obtaining insurance against any accidents that might befall me during my one-day visit, I make my way early to the corner of Jackson Boulevard and La Salle Street. The appointment is for 8.30, an hour before trading begins. Outside the building, dozens of traders stand drinking from obligatory paper cups of coffee, waiting to get stuck into their working day. They look burdened, but authentic, a lot less artificial than their colleagues in suits and ties that populate the temple of finance in Wall Street. They are mostly big American boys from the Midwest, middle-class rednecks who often do this job not through any great passion or because they want to be rich, but just to get by. They are, I'm about to discover, simple soldiers in a war fought every day in the *pits* where they buy and sell. The Generals are up on the high floors, sitting in armchairs, giving orders to the troops via earpieces. Or else further away, planning purchasing and selling strategies on the basis of mathematical models.

The Director for Media Contacts comes to meet me at reception. She's a cold lady with a sharp face and a sullen smile. After introducing ourselves, she quickly but efficiently explains to me how I should behave. I may film for half an hour, from 9.30 to 10. I am authorised to mingle among the traders, but without interfering in the negotiations. Any questions I have I must put to Vic Lespinasse, an expert dealer who will come down to the hall at 9.45 to give me fifteen minutes of his time. She thanks me for coming and leaves me in the hands of an intern from Colorado, who moves a little clumsily through the rooms. 'I've only been here two weeks', she says, smiling, 'and I've already seen seven TV crews from all over the world.' What goes on here is in the news; the Chicago stock market is in the eye of the cyclone. Journalists have descended en masse to the scene of the crime.

We enter the arena. The *grain* room – dealing in basic food products, corn, soya, grain, rice, etc. – is about 3,000 square metres in size. In the middle of the room hundreds of dealers are amiably chatting away to each other. Some are wearing green bibs. Others are dressed in blue, red, purple shirts. They have little yellow cards where the front pocket should be, indicating which group they belong to. It looks more like a carnival show than the inside of a stock market where the value of basic food products is decided and will determine food prices across the planet.

At 9.30 on the dot, the bell rings. A yell crosses the floor like a massive roar. A picture of calm just a few seconds ago, now the traders go wild. They race for the pits. They shout. They gesticulate wildly, throwing their arms about in a frenzy. They hold pieces of paper, rip them up, throw the pieces into the air. To look at them from a distance, without knowing the codes that are used for negotiations, you would think they're all suffering convulsions from tarantula bites. In fact, their hand movements are following precise rules: a sign with the palm faced towards his body means that the trader wants to buy. Vice versa, the palm facing outwards means he wants to sell. With his fingers towards his face he signals how much he wants to buy or sell, and so on according to coded gestures that seem more like shamanic spells than stock-market transactions.

Up on high, on a notice board that covers the four sides of the hall like a sort of digital ceiling, the variations in the value of the merchandise can be read in real time. In the centre, a large screen shows the weather forecast for around the world: a flood in the Ukraine will be an incentive to immediately buy futures in grain, before the price gets too high. A sunny spell on Mato Grosso could be a good sign for the soya harvest and will signal the operators to sell.

The dealings continue without a pause. A man yells something and twists his hand, possibly unsure whether to sell or to buy. He writes something on a piece of paper. Then he reconsiders, and with a theatrical gesture he rips the paper into several pieces, before banging his fist against his temples. Another man beside him laughs. Another grimaces in desperation. Practically the same scene is repeated across the pits. The big hall seems like a collection of many little boxing rings, and when the gong sounds at 9.30 hundreds of simultaneous fights start. The dealers fight without looking at each other, because each of them is fighting by himself against everybody else. His victory or defeat won't be determined by a referee or by the dealer beside him, but by the numbers on the board that gradually show the price a bushel of grain or corn is heading towards. As the exchanges continue, the quoted prices change incessantly, and the upward looks from the dealers lead to a variety of responses from dismay to euphoria. Most of the dealers will buy, sell and re-buy the same merchandise many times over the course of the day, in an attempt to profit from the variations in price as negotiations proceed. None of them are actually interested in the purchase of soya, grain or corn. It's quite likely that a good proportion of them have never even seen a bushel of these agricultural products. They are playing with numbers and with their instincts. And it will be those instincts, combined with the indications they'll eventually receive from their colleagues on the higher floors, that will determine whether they walk away from the daily battle as losers or victors. In this fight to the death, the towel is only thrown in at 13.30, when, after four hours of open or closed hands, shredded paper, and incomprehensible shouts, the dealers will count their winnings or losses and go to the cafeteria under the skyscraper to lick their wounds or celebrate the spoils they've raked in.

'We are a thermometer'

Two different species of animal sweat it out in the pits: on the one hand there are the employees of the large brokerage houses, who buy and sell for others, such as big agribusiness groups, producer cooperatives, but also pension funds, speculative funds or other investors keen on diversifying their portfolio. Some of these salaried traders are highly motivated. Others already seem to be suffering from the kind of alienation typical of those who do repetitive work. They buy and sell by following orders, at times they hardly know what goods they are dealing in. This is brought home to me when I cross paths with a trader at the end of his working day. It's just after two o'clock when the man comes out of the stock market. He looks exhausted. He obviously can't wait to go home. 'What did you buy today?' I ask him. 'Soya,' he answers. 'And what did you sell?' 'Soya.' 'Why?' 'I don't know.'

Beside the salaried workers, there are also single dealers. These are pure gamblers who live on stress and adrenalin, suspended each day somewhere between bankruptcy and paradise. But these kind of dealers have almost all abandoned the pit hall. They play on their computer, at home, buying and selling at their pleasure at whatever time of day or night. Because the great trading floor of the Chicago stock market, with its gestured negotiations, its pieces of paper and its bibs, is by now an anachronism. Most of the trading is no longer done here, but electronically, and continues twenty-four hours a day. Trading from 9.30 to 13.30 continues only as a form of representation, the visible sign of a phenomenon whose substance lies elsewhere, in the virtually limitless recesses of cyberspace.

It is in these recesses, rather than in among the risk-takers who physically exert themselves in the pits, that the cause for the increase in primary food futures or food commodities is to be found. As mentioned in the previous chapter, it all started – or accelerated – in the summer of 2007. The sub-prime mortgage crisis fell like an avalanche on the United States economy, destroying consolidated groups with glorious pasts. In the space of a few months a string of semi-governmental agencies go bust: Freddie Mac and Fanny Mae, the insurance colossus AIG and the financial conglomerates Lehman Brothers, Merrill Lynch, Washington Mutual, Wachovia and Citygroup. The explosion of the property bubble brings to the fore many toxic derivative products, which like a virus infect stock markets around the world. The shares market deflates. Investors cut their losses and pull out, turning instead to so-called 'refuge goods': gold, silver and primary food goods. The price of grain futures shoots through the roof, causing a rise in prices throughout the entire production line: between 2006 and 2008 the prices of grain and rice on the world market increases by 136 percent and 217 percent respectively, with transitory leaps that push the price up by as much as 150 percent in the space of a couple of weeks.[6] The basic food products used by the poor – such as rice and bread – rise in many parts of the world. There is a widespread outbreak of 'hunger riots', from Egypt to the Ivory Coast and from Haiti to the Philippines. It is at this point that the Chicago Board of Trade ends up in the dock, since it is here and no place else that the reference values of basic food goods is decided for whoever in the world wants to buy or sell them. It is also from here that the anomalous wave began which shook the entire world. But are the speculators entirely to blame?

Vic Lespinasse, the expert trader who has been given the task of explaining the market mechanisms to me, certainly doesn't think so. Lespinasse is a Chicago Board of Trade veteran, having arrived there fresh in the 1970s with an economics degree in his pocket and a burning desire to make good as a dealer. In the grain room he is considered an institution, a fact brought home to me by the constant respectful greetings he receives from his younger colleagues.

Slender, with a drooping moustache and clear blue eyes, he has been chosen as spokesman for the traders in their dealings with the barrage of journalists now flocking to the stock market to get the full story. And he is perfect for the role. Lespinasse knows his stuff. He always thinks before answering. He never says too much. And there isn't an ounce of uncertainty in what he says. 'There's no such thing as a speculative bubble,' he begins. 'The prices of primary food products are rising because of a series of economic elements: bad harvests, an increase in consumption in emerging countries such as China and India, a rise in biofuel production, implying a rise in lands designated for the cultivation of corn not for consumption. All of these elements cause the traders to bet on price rises and the market to ferment. It's ridiculous to say that it's the traders who are causing the price increases. We simply don't have this kind of power. We're like a thermometer: we measure the market's temperature. If we think that demand is going to be greater than supply, we buy, because we figure prices are going to rise. If it's the opposite, we sell.'

Is this merely the official line of defence from a representative of a group under fire, or is it the calm rationale of a man who has spent his life trading in basic food produce? It's hard to say: the truth is probably somewhere in between. I point out to him that if Chicago is a thermometer, then it is probably measuring the temperature of an environment which has been overheated by an enormous influx of capital coming from a shares market in free-fall. As I'm saying this, a shout rings out across the hall: the price of corn has just reached a new record, 7.2 dollars a bushel. Hands are raised. Whistles ring out. Sheets of paper are ripped to shreds. Lespinasse doesn't bat an eyelid. 'It's been happening a lot lately', he says with a little smile. Then he carries right on: 'It's true, recently there has been an enormous influx of speculative funds here in Chicago, because the shares market is not doing well but the commodity market is. So the speculator's money is being pumped into the commodity market. But I believe that speculators follow trends that have already been established, and that these trends would occur in any case. I don't think it's the speculators who cause an increase in prices. They may have partly contributed, but overall their input is fairly insignificant.'

The question at the heart of the subject now dominating the news is this: Are the speculators following a trend or are they creating it? In other words: is the increase in the price of basic food products caused by market elements or by a new speculative bubble created by reckless investors gambling on massive profits for themselves or their clients? Everyone at the Chicago stock market, from the Director to the janitor and Lespinasse in between, is ready to swear that they are not responsible. They say that their powers don't reach that far. The stock market doesn't cause the fever, it measures it.

The metaphor of the 'thermometer' is on everybody's lips. It's repeated like a mantra by several of the traders I meet at the end of the session. It's also repeated to me by Patrick Arbor, the king of the Chicago Board of Trade, the prince of negotiation, the grain wizard, to list just a few of nicknames he's been given by the press over the years. Arbor is the person who best represents the history of the Chicago stock market, of which he has been Director for three consecutive mandates, totalling six years. Active in the field as far back as 1965, today he runs an investment company – Arbor Investments Inc. – whose headquarters is located in the same skyscraper as the stock market. The front of the Arbor office is a gigantic entrance with floor-to-ceiling glass walls that look down onto the street. It's bright, spacious, welcoming. It's obvious that Arbor and the group that takes his name look at the world from up on high, proud of the success they have achieved.

After a few minutes' wait I am accompanied into the boss's office, a cramped little room with a desk to one side on which books and folders are stacked in moderate disorder. Behind it, a screen which is always tuned to CNBC – a cable channel specialising in business. The effect is disorientating, the contradiction too striking: the airy and bright ambiance of the waiting room jars with this eight-metre squared room, lit by neon and furnished with two distinctly common chairs. It's like passing, in the space of one corridor, from the headquarters of a billionaire group to the office of a provincial accountant. And yet, on reflection, this has probably been specifically designed. The layout of space would seem to follow a very precise logic. The offices are cramped because they are strictly workplaces, not for idling about in. The reception rooms, on the other hand, are spacious and comfortable, because this is where the clients are brought, and the clients must feel at ease with and reassured by the company in which they are investing their money. Whoever comes here to visit must first take notice where this group has got to, and then understand how it got there. He must understand, in Arbor's own words, a trader's ultimate goal: 'to accumulate something every day, without giving in to greed' and 'to get to such great heights without suffering from vertigo'.

Arbor is a climber, in every sense of the word. He started off at the stock market as a simple trader and has ended high up, so high up that he can adopt the following philosophy: 'We believe that we have reached such great heights so that we can see further into the distance,' as he writes on his group's website.[7] But Arbor is also a passionate mountaineer. He has scaled mountains of more than five thousand metres, all over the world. The walls of his office are covered with evidence of these glorious feats: in one photo he is seen giving the victory sign on top of Mount Kilimanjaro, in another he looks more tired as he stands at the peak of Mont Blanc. I study the photos with curiosity, asking Arbor for details of where and when.

Then one photo in particular grabs my attention. I see Patrick in a dark suit, in the company of the musician and showman, Renzo Arbore. 'He's my cousin,' he says. I look at him, bewildered. He starts to explain: 'My grandfather was an Italian who came to the Midwest to make his fortune. His name was Savino Arbore. Soon after arriving in Chicago, he was killed during an argument that broke out with some unseemly characters. His family then decided it was time for a change of surname, time to make it more American. And so the *e* was dropped. Many years later I came to Florence to learn your beautiful language. Someone there pointed out to me that I vaguely resembled Renzo Arbore who, like my grandfather, was also from Puglia. I contacted him, we met and we traced our common roots. Ever since, we've seen each other quite a bit.' 'That photo', he says, pointing to the picture that had caught my attention, 'was taken here in Chicago.'

Patrick has a tapered face that ends in a very neat white goatee, which matches what little smooth hair remains on his temples. He is thin, with a sleek physique. He's got a low, not very expansive voice, and talks calmly while looking straight into your eyes. When I come into his room, he looks me up and down, tells me to sit and asks me which city 'in our *bel paese*' I hail from. Before our interview begins, he insists on showing me something. He logs on to YouTube and chooses a video: a documentary entitled *Gravina Hours*. It's an amateur video: the camerawork is shaky, the picture a little out of focus. The film shows a medieval procession, with dressed-up horses, jockeys carrying banners, knights wearing armour. Then the scene cuts to the town square, where the camera focuses on an old clock. And here we see – or rather can just about make out, as the picture quality is terrible – a well-dressed man in modern clothes. It's Patrick, drawing back the inauguration curtain. The clock, which hadn't worked for fifty years, has been restored thanks to his financial support. Arbor was keeping a promise he had made the previous year, when he received honorary citizenship of the town, after discovering that his grandmother had emigrated from there. The words he says in Italian are: 'It was about time that this clock started working again.'

This episode may not seem all that significant, but it gives a good idea of the man. Arbor respects tradition. Born and raised in Chicago, part of a poor immigrant Italian family, he made his own way in the ferocious world of traders. He has gone far – or rather, 'high' – and he doesn't hide this. As a successful man, he wants to rekindle the traditions of his far-off place of origin. But he is even more attached to the place that has graced him, the city where he was born, raised and where he made his fortune. He can't stand that the name of the Chicago Board of Trade, to which he has dedicated such a large part of his life, is being muddied as we speak. 'Today the talk is of speculators who are starving the planet,' he says in a measured tone. 'But this doesn't make any sense. We're just a stock market. We don't decide prices, it's the buyers and sellers who do that. What's more, we have precise laws for protecting the market whenever rules are not being respected. If some-body does something underhand, we suspend trading, and can even expel him.' Then he takes a moment's breath and unfurls the password phrase, the omnipresent explanation that I've already heard a hundred times in the last few days. 'The market is fluctuating because of changes in the real economy. We are just the thermometer that measures these fluctuations.'

'Yes, but recently there has been a great influx of money into the commodities market, which has certainly distorted prices,' I argue.

'That's true up to a point. These commodities are in fact new financial products upon which pension funds in America and in other parts of the world have depended in order to protect themselves. One, two or three percent of these funds' capital is invested in the commodities market. These funds are constantly present on the market, from month to month, because they have an obligation. They have to provide returns to their subscribers and protect them from inflation. And so they've relied on refuge goods, such as oil, corn, soya. Having said that, to assert that European or American pensioners have raised the price of bread by investing in Chicago is just plain far-fetched.'

'But can't the influx of fresh money drug the market?'

'Whoever bets on futures does so in the light of real data', Arbor insists. 'There is no puppet master raking in all the futures of a particular product in order to shoot up the price. There's no speculative bubble on cereals. If there were, it would have burst by now.'

'If the stock market is a meeting place for buyers and sellers, how many contracts actually end with a delivery of goods?'

'Very few, perhaps 1 percent,' responds Arbor. 'But that's always been the way. The speculators' role is to circulate liquidity and to permit what we call in technical jargon *hedging*, or the protection of the section by the operators, who take on a role in the financial market that is opposite to the one they have in the real economy. Markets need speculation. It's not a bad word. Without speculators, who assume the risk, hedging wouldn't be possible and the market wouldn't work.'

In layman's terms, speculators bet on what is going to happen to the price, which lets the line operators (agricultural retailers, food product wholesalers, first transformers) undertake hedging. The speculators can make or lose money, depending on whether their prediction is right or wrong. Those who practice hedging, on the other hand, can be certain they won't lose money, because whatever they lose on the stock market they'll make up in the real economy and vice versa. If there were no speculators – and therefore if the value of futures didn't vary – the market would be more unstable.

But if the presence and increase of speculation guarantees more security for the sector's operators, a rise in prices has repercussions on a global level and for consumers throughout the planet, who see the cost of their food go up. Arbor is on this point categorical: 'That has nothing to do with us. The increase in the price of cereal is determined by structural elements, by the market,' he repeats once again. Then, repeating Lespinasse's words almost verbatim, he starts to list what he believes to be the factors that have led to the upsurge in food prices: 'There's greater consumption of meat in countries such as China and India, which increases the demand for animal feed. There's the increase in oil prices. There have been a run of bad harvests. And there have certainly been foolish policies, such as that of the United States' administration to promote the development of biofuels from corn.'

Iowa, the American Kuwait
The US policy on biofuels is the other major defendant in the case against the planets' hunger merchants. For the past few years, the United States has been implementing a programme of incentives for the development of 'green fuels', particularly ethanol produced from corn. The race for ethanol was officially launched by the former President George W. Bush in his 2006 State of the Union speech. After declaring that America's main problem is its dependence on oil ('America is addicted to oil'), the President announced heavy investment in the production of biofuels, together with other forms of 'clean energy'.

With the legislation proposed by Bush and approved by Congress, the US committed itself to increasing sevenfold the amount of ethanol available at the pumps by 2022. A stimulant for production came on top of federal subsidies already given to companies that distribute ethanol to the pumps of 51 cents per gallon, later reduced to 45.[8] The main reason that spurred an administration so traditionally linked with the oil companies to go down this road was a geo-strategic one. As Bush openly admitted: 'Our aim is to transform our dependence on Middle East oil, which in the case of many countries is unreliable, into a thing of the past.' In fact, the objective is twofold: to reduce dependence on crude oil from the Middle East (but also from Venezuela), and to satisfy the strong agricultural lobby in the Midwest.[9]

Following Bush's speech, ethanol factories sprang up like mushrooms throughout the US corn belt, extending from Illinois to Wyoming and including Iowa, Nebraska and South Dakota. Iowa is in fact the leading biofuel producer in the country: the state numbers thirty-three factories which annually produce more than three billion gallons of ethanol,[10] over a quarter of the total amount produced in the entire country.[11]

Here the farmers have organised. They've formed cooperatives. They've created pressure groups. And they've established powerful synergies: the one for corn producers (the Iowa Corn Growers Association), and the one for ethanol producers (Iowa Renewable Fuels Association) work side-by-side to spread the word about biofuels and apply the right pressure in Washington so that the policy of offering incentives stays in place. They even have their headquarters in the same building, further testament to their common interests. When I contact both press offices, they give me the same answer and the same appointment. 'Come to the Indy Car Series at Newton next Sunday. All the members of our association will be there.'

Newton is a backward town in the middle of the Interstate 80, the highway that works its way right across the United States. Identical to a thousand other small towns without a history that line the roadside of the highway, its layout is that of a transit town: a handful of motels, a couple of bars and a few service stations with adjoining restaurants. There's no real centre to speak of. The town spreads horizontally to the right of the highway. On the left, the circuit has been built for the Indy Car Series, the race that is holding a stage in Iowa. A very timely stage, given that in 2007 the organisers decided to introduce an important new feature: all the race cars run on ethanol.

An enormous banner welcomes the lines of visitors that scramble for a spot in the improvised car park beside the circuit: 'Welcome to the only race in the world that uses renewable fuel.' Hundreds of people line up for tickets, the gazebos outside the track are packed to capacity, the terraces full to the brim. Families, farmers, sponsors, curious onlookers: the race is an authentic celebration. But it's not just a simple sporting event. It is also and primarily a gigantic ethanol fair. Many stands are set up to champion the qualities of this fuel, which 'doesn't pollute, is renewable and, most importantly, is American'. Grilled corn is handed out. A man dressed as a giant corncob bobs among the crowd. 'Hi, I'm Mr Corn!' he says to the intrigued children drawn to him. Another man wears the mask of a fuel pump that supplies E85 – 85 percent ethanol, 15 percent petrol. A little further down, at the Renewable Fuels Association stand, a race car has been parked so that children can play in it. While the smaller ones drive at the wheel, their parents are being updated on the advantages of ethanol and the latest developments. A girl from the Association explains the speed at which 'green fuel' pumps are being opened in the United States. 'Last Sunday we were in Atlanta, Georgia, and in a single day we inaugurated twelve E85 stations. By now, ethanol has spread beyond the Midwest.'

The race cars – the girl explains – run on 98 percent ethanol. Two percent of gas is added because a US law forbids fuel from being 100 percent alcohol, 'to avoid human consumption', she says in a serious tone. I try in vain to imagine a line of alcoholics taking their bottles to the pumps only to desist because of that 2 percent of petrol.

I make my way down the side of the racetrack to the area reserved for journalists. Behind the bleachers there are drivers, managers and sponsors. I see Marco Andretti, the most popular Italian-American driver of the moment, the son and grandson of famous pilots in time gone by. He is also endorsing the ethanol car race. A swarm of fans surround him as he signs autographs and shakes hands. Some of his colleagues are trying on their helmets and listening to the last snippets of advice from their respective managers, before preparing themselves at the starting blocks. A few minutes later the race begins. The cars are off. They gain speed. They start hustling around the little track, accompanied by the screams of the radio announcer, who dedicates every third phrase to praising the firepower of the new fuel. 'It's amazing. It's efficient. It's American.' The drivers skid along the circuit, which is incredibly short but with many bends. The fans roar on the terraces, armed with binoculars through which they try to get a peek of their idols. The race cars are neck and neck, reaching speeds of 200 mph on the straights. 'Ethanol', the announcer proclaims, 'gives the same performance as normal gas.' The noise, the smell, the cheering of the fans, are like those of a Formula One race. In the end, after two hours of racing and drama, including all the pit stops and accidents, Andretti qualifies in third place.

I follow the race on a small TV screen in the prefab being used as a media office. Beside me is a group of farmers from the Iowa Corn Growers Association. We're all sitting around a circular table. We introduce ourselves. The first one – Dean – starts to speak. He's a giant of a man – he must be two metres tall and weigh 130 kilos. The Association's blue T-shirt he's wearing does little to hide a robust body that's not exactly all muscle. 'For the first time in years we're not making a loss. The increase in the price of corn is like a breath of fresh air for us. All of this is part of a system that makes more sense: we produce corn, which is sold at a higher price. That corn is used to produce ethanol, which means we don't have to import oil from regimes that aren't too friendly with the United States. This way, the national economy grows and we also guarantee ourselves energy independence.' This logic would be watertight if the US policy wasn't disrupting the cereal market worldwide and thus having far-reaching repercussions.

'We're sorry that there are hunger riots in Africa,' adds Tim, a short, stocky farmer, in a quiet voice, 'but the accusations against us are spurious. We didn't cause the rise in prices. We just sell our produce. If the price rises it's because of speculators.'

'Yes, but speculators buy futures because they know there's going to be more and more need for corn, not least because of the policy on ethanol,' I argue.

'We're producing more corn than before. It's not true that there's less corn on the market. A part of what we produce is for ethanol, a part for human and animal consumption,' says another.

'And anyway', says Dean, 'we're importing oil, so we don't control it. We're producing the ethanol here at home: this policy isn't just good for the Midwest and for the producing states, but for the entire country.' The question of energy independence is a very sensitive one in the US, which lives with the persistent fear of one day finding itself without any fuel. Dean the giant continues his line of reasoning with an analogy that works quite well: 'Iowa is the Kuwait of America, and we are the Arabs of the Midwest.' At this, his friends and colleagues nod their heads. They seem convinced. They're not just happy to see their profits rise. They also believe they're doing a service to their nation: freeing America from its dependence on oil.

But if the Iowa farmers number among ethanol's biggest fans, renewable fuel is not to everybody's liking. Its effect on the price of corn has created a division across the country that goes beyond simple party affiliations and resembles that of the War of Secession: the Southern states, whose economies are based on livestock breeding and have therefore been burnt by the rise in the price of corn, argue that the ethanol incentives have hurt them badly. At the height of the crisis, in the summer of 2008, the Governor of Texas Richard Perry wrote a caustic open letter in which he asked Congress to eliminate or at least reduce the subsidies.[12] California introduced a law on emission reduction that heavily penalised ethanol.[13] As senator for Arizona, and later as a (defeated) candidate at the 2008 presidential election, John McCain has always argued for the necessity of eliminating subsidies for agrofuels. His rival and the present tenant of the White House, the Democrat Barack Obama, has, on the other hand, always been strenuously in favour. And he has openly admitted that the reason is geographical: 'I'm a strong supporter of ethanol because Illinois is a large producer of corn,'[14] he has said on several occasions.[15]

At the height of the crisis and the hunger riots in 2008, the debate takes a somewhat schematic form along the 'food-fuel' dichotomy. Ethanol, according to its detractors, removes corn from food consumption and denies arable land to other types of cultivation. This produces food scarcity. The thesis is supported by a World Bank study according to which 75 percent of the food crisis is attributable to agrofuels.[16] The two sides – pro-ethanol and anti-ethanol – fight it out using adverts, scientific studies, and conflicting lobbying manoeuvres. For one study that shows how ethanol contributes to a reduction in petrol prices, another will be advanced by its opponents that shows the exact opposite – and that ethanol is really a con because its production requires fossil-fuel energy to cultivate the fields and power the refineries.[17] Research demonstrating that productivity in the fields has increased because of the subsidies is opposed by other research arguing that to provide the amount of energy the United States needs it would be necessary to grow corn across the entire western hemisphere.[18]

When one examines the two sides of the debate, the argument in favour of ethanol doesn't really stand up: the only people defending it seem to be the farmers in the Midwest and the politicians representing them. Those who, in theory, should have welcomed it with open arms, such as the environmentalists, almost immediately threw their lot in with its opponents, maintaining that it is completely illegitimate to define ethanol as a 'green fuel'. The head of this school of thought is undoubtedly Lester Brown. The Director of the Earth Policy Institute, a Washington environmental think-tank, the man is a bona fide guru of sustainable development. Defined by the *Washington Post* as 'one of the most influential thinkers in the world', he has received twenty-four honorary degrees over the course of his career. He has published around fifty books that have defined, over the years, a bold eco-economy project, a plan of campaign for reducing waste and inefficiency and saving the planet. Described in detail in his book *Plan B 3.0*, his project has no place for biofuels. In fact, he considers them a total misfortune. When I meet him in Rome, at the presentation of the Italian version of his book,[19] I find him a modest man of about seventy, with ruffled grey hair, a creased jacket and a pair of white running shoes that have seen better days. Brown has the dreamy air of a '68 militant who is now getting on a bit. He moves awkwardly between the TV cameras filming him and smiles a little tiredly at the photo sessions the press demand of him. He's bored, and it shows. I get the impression that at any moment he'll find some excuse to absent himself, jump into a taxi and get as far away as humanly possible. As soon as he begins to speak, however, his brusque manner gives way to the force of his arguments. He speaks with an encyclopaedic knowledge of the subject in hand, citing facts and figures at will, and rattling off calculations. 'The transfer of corn to ethanol production is creating a problem on a world scale. This year in the American Midwest, a quarter of the 400 million tonnes of corn produced was set aside for fuel production as opposed to consumption. This has created an imbalance, given that stocks have diminished. Seven of the past eight years have registered a deficit in cereal production, and reserves worldwide have plummeted to their lowest level in the past thirty-four years. So prices have shot up. Over the past two years at the Chicago Board of Trade, corn has more than doubled in price. There is one main reason for this increase: the euphoria for ethanol that has struck producers in the Midwest, not least because of the generous subsidies provided by the federal government.'

I respond with the energy independence argument so popular among the Iowa farmers. 'That argument has no basis in fact,' he contends. 'It should be remembered that, even if all of the arable land in the United States was used to produce corn for ethanol, it would still only provide barely 16 percent of the fuel demands of American consumers. Not to mention that the energy balance of ethanol is extremely low: for every unit of energy used for producing it, the outcome is only 1.3 units.'

From his commanding position, Brown has to some extent assumed the role of spokesman for the 'food against fuel' position. 'There's competition between 800 million people with cars and 800 million who are risking starvation,' he says solemnly. 'We're at a fork in the road: in order to save a little on our car habit we are starving millions of people in the southern hemisphere. It's time to face facts: are we really prepared to commit such a crime?'

'No soldiers to defend the fields'

The arguments made by Lester Brown are by no means uncommon. In many parts of the world, voices of protest against agrofuels are now resounding like a loud and polyphonic chorus. Livestock breeders, environmentalists, farming organisations, experts and officials are questioning to various degrees the efficiency of ethanol and of the biodiesel extracted from soya and palm oil. They link the development of this fuel with the food price increases and stigmatise (albeit in different tones) the incentives policy adopted by the United States and, to some extent, Brazil, where ethanol is extracted from sugar-cane, which at least has a much better energy balance than the figure quoted by Lester Brown. Images of big American SUVs are placed alongside others of malnourished children around the world. A large part of the 2008 FAO summit on food sovereignty was dedicated to the relation between these new fuels and the rise in food prices. In the end, as so often happens at these summits, nothing was decided. The final document merely included a general recommendation on the need to 'undertake detailed studies to ensure that the production and use of biofuels adequately takes into consideration the neces-sity of guaranteeing and maintaining world food security'.[20]

In this climate of growing and generalised hostility, US producers are feeling unfairly blamed for things that are not their fault. And they are circling the wagons. When I ask the Iowa Renewable Fuels Association to organise a visit for me to one of the state's ethanol factories, they send me a list of refin-eries and the contact details of the people running them. 'You call them, see if they're available.' A little surprised at this lack of cooperation, I faithfully begin a round of phone calls, only to come up against a seemingly impenetrable wall. Some tell me to send them an email, an email they will never answer. Others answer that it is not part of their policy to organise visits for reporters. One in particular, who I have spent the entire day chasing down, finally tells me in an outburst of sincerity that 'at this time we've decided to keep a low profile, at least until the storm passes. This is why we prefer not to talk to the media.' When I have just about given up, after dozens of emails and phone calls, I decide to make one final desperate attempt and call the last factory on the list. I dial the number and repeat what has by now become my standard mantra: 'Hello, I'm a reporter undertaking a study on biofuels, and I would like to visit your factory to understand the potential and the advantages of your product.' I say this phrase mechanically, without enthusiasm, jaded by the stream of *No*'s I'd been met with up to this point. On the other end of the line, a very kind-sounding lady says: 'When would you like to come?' For a moment I can't speak for the shock. Then, stuttering with surprise, I tell her the dates I'm going to be in the state the following week and that any day for me is just fine. So we make an appointment.

The factory is in West Burlington, a sleepy town on the border of Iowa and Illinois, just a stone's throw from the mighty Mississippi river that separates the two states. The refinery is unmistakeable: a steel complex that rises out of the surrounding green fields like a gigantic futurist cathedral. At its entrance, an orderly line of trucks waits to unload the corn. I make my way to reception and meet the lady I had spoken to on the phone. She asks me to wait just a few minutes, because her boss is on his lunch break. 'He'll be right along,' she says, before heading off to lunch herself. 'You won't need me. I'm sure you'll recognise Mr Defenbaugh when you see him.'

Sure enough, a few minutes later a white Volkswagen beetle pulls into the park in front of the office. It's a new model with personalised licence plates that have seven letters: ETHANOL. The car door opens, and out steps a two-metre giant with a white beard that flows down to his chest.

Ray Defenbaugh has remarkably blue eyes from which spring a lively intelligence, a voice so guttural that it seems to come straight from the stomach, and an explosive laugh that reverberates like a drum. He greets me with a vigorous handshake and, having received my compliments on his car, sets about telling me its performance statistics. 'Of course, it's not exactly common here in the Midwest. Most people around here go for SUVs. This here is a European car. With one difference: it's an E85, runs on 85 percent ethanol. Where you're from, these cars don't exist.' Only after I've been talking to him for a few minutes do I notice something that, somehow, I hadn't noticed before: the man only has one arm. His right arm ends at the elbow in a stump, which he nonetheless moves as if his arm were intact. He neither hides it nor vaunts it. He just uses it as if it were a normal limb. At one point, to show me where a warehouse is, he says 'It's over there,' pointing with the stump. This is why his disability goes unnoticed and, judging by what he gets done, may in fact be no disability at all. Throughout the many hours I spend with him in the factory I never manage to ask him when and how he lost his arm. Perhaps it's because I'm afraid the answer's going to be 'Lost my arm? What are you talking about?'

Defenbaugh is extremely informal. He invites me for a coffee. 'If you'd come a little earlier I would've taken you to lunch at a place I know. To eat real Midwest meat,' he says amicably. Dressed in a fairly tattered pair of jeans, with a white T-shirt under a checked shirt, he looks more like a farmer than the Executive Director of one of Iowa's leading ethanol factories. 'We're a small cooperative of farmers and small investors from this area. A few years ago we got together and decided it was worth it to give this adventure a shot. The factory produces a hundred million gallons a year, used throughout the Midwest. We opened in 2005, and our turnover's been increasing ever since,' he says, stroking his beard.

Two types of investors have gone into the production of ethanol from corn: large multinational groups (such as Archer Daniels Midland, based in Illinois, who control a large part of the world's cereal market) and cooperatives of farmers and investors. The factory run by Defenbaugh belongs to this second category. He expounds upon the ethical principles that moved him and his partners to open it: 'Ethanol is good for many reasons. It allows us to increase the value of merchandise that we grow a lot in abundance here: corn. We were producing so much corn that the sale price was lower than the production price. There was no future in this. By making ethanol from corn, we have increased our children's chances for survival here, it gives them the chance to work in the fields again, and it offers the possibility to get enough capital to build the kind of infrastructure that the factories need.'

He continues, this time looking beyond the Iowa prairies and adopting a more geopolitical perspective. 'You've travelled on our roads. What have you seen? Corn, corn, corn. That's all the Midwest is. We have the corn and we can produce the fuel: from one acre of land we can produce over 500 gallons of ethanol. When you drive through Illinois and Iowa, you see these thousands and thousands of acres of land on which corn is growing. But not one soldier. All that ethanol and there's not even one soldier to defend those fields. You never see a young man or woman coming back in a plastic bag because they were defending those fields. So I say: why do we have to send our kids to protect oil fields in Iraq, only to see them die, instead of producing our own fuel right here, in peace and tranquillity?' Ray is on a roll now. As he takes me on a long tour around the factory, he talks endlessly, with that bellowing voice of his that outdoes even the machinery. He shows me where the corn is unloaded. He takes a handful of corn, studies it, weighs up its quality. He points out the various phases of its transformation, shows me the tanks where the distillation takes place, reels off technical details on the refining process. He takes me to the lab, where every last phase of production is being followed by the computer system. Then he hands me the end product: a small bottle of ethanol, colourless, transparent, without a definable odour. He looks at it with a smile: 'This is the future, make no bones about it. The oil is going to run out. Corn, by its very definition, won't: it's renewable.' This man is a pioneer. He started producing agrofuels when nobody believed in them. And now he is rejecting all the criticism. 'A couple of weeks ago, a TV crew came here from Al Jazeera. They spent three days in the factory. We were together ten hours a day. And for three days they kept asking me the same question: don't you know that what you're doing here is causing the starvation of millions of people around the planet?'

This, of course, was the exact same question I was preparing to ask him. I let him go on. 'These criticisms are false and unfair. The rise in food prices is due to many factors, including increases in oil prices and distribution systems. We're just a small variable within a much larger mechanism, which we of all people certainly don't govern.'

'Many people argue that ethanol only works because of the incentives and that the energy balance of this fuel is totally unsatisfactory', I point out. 'They say ethanol isn't efficient. That production costs are higher than the returns. If that's true, it doesn't explain why we are still in business,' he rages. 'Nor does it explain why everybody is building ethanol factories, not just in the Midwest but throughout the United States.'

It's true that the policy of subsidies doesn't directly favour producers, but the companies that sell the fuel at the pumps. However, cause-effect relations are often difficult to govern: the subsidies increase demand, and this increases the amount of land given over to corn as opposed to other crops, thus raising the prices of the latter; importing countries suffer from these price hikes; third world populations go hungry and take to the streets to protest. The small variable Defenbaugh speaks of can influence the mechanism and cause it to flounder.

An integrated system
Upon returning to Chicago, the system of variables is explained to me in a precise, almost didactic way by a young trader who I meet by chance at the stock market café. I'm

drinking my coffee and waiting for a sandwich. The young man sits down beside me. He's clean-faced and clearly from a good family, with a square face, blond hair and a pair of small glasses that give him a very professional air. He can't be more than twenty-eight. 'Bad day?' he asks as he takes his seat. 'I'm just visiting. I'm a reporter,' I answer. His face lights up. 'And what do you make of what goes on here?' 'I'm trying to understand the link between agrofuels, speculation and the food crisis.'

'Aw, that's old hat,' he answers. 'Want me to explain it to you?' Without waiting for an answer, he takes a serviette and starts frenetically scribbling diagrams. He draws squares. In one he writes *corn*, in another *wheat*, in another, *soya bean*. Between the squares he draws some arrows. At the top of the arrow pointing towards corn he writes *biofuel*. From the corn square, the arrow points towards wheat, from which another arrow points vertically up.

'It works like this,' he starts to explain. 'Now everybody wants corn, that's the hot product at the moment. But it's already late for corn: corn should've been bought before, when the market was less crowded. Every commodity is part of a system. If oil goes up and people start talking about agrofuels, everybody buys corn. But in the meantime, there's going to be something smaller like wheat whose price will go up, simply because the land where wheat has been grown is now going to be used for corn, for ethanol, for biofuels. So there's going to be less wheat, and it's going to be worth more. Whoever has any money should buy wheat.' 'Is that what you bought today?' I ask him. 'I bought soya, because today there was a chance to earn something there. But I don't work for myself. I'm an employee, what they call a trader for rent. They give me a little cash and I have to make it grow in a very small time-frame. But if I could and if I had my own funds, I'd invest in something else.' 'In what?' 'Personally, I believe that the investment of the future isn't primary goods, but land. Primary goods will be subject to small speculations that'll provide a chance to earn from short-term variations in the futures. The real investment, with guaranteed and probably much greater returns, will be land, especially in countries where exploitation and production costs hardly anything. Right now primary goods are on the boil, but this won't last forever. It's a heck of a lot safer and more lucrative to invest in land.'

In the months following my trip to the American Midwest, the situation has indeed changed. The prices of primary food goods have fallen, albeit not to the levels they were at before the 2007 crisis. Oil prices have dropped a little, which makes investment in ethanol less attractive. The crisis in the banking sector has reduced the amount of loans being offered, which has forced many companies who have turned to agrofuel production to downsize their objectives or even close down altogether. In short, if the bubble hasn't burst it has certainly deflated quite a bit. And the big investors have shifted their attention to something even more tangible than primary food goods: land, the most basic good of all, a safe and profitable investment.

In short, everything has gone exactly as that young Chicago trader predicted, and if he has managed to convince someone to give him some cash, he might now be enjoying the fruits of his bullseye prediction somewhere a lot more exotic than the café under the Chicago Board of Trade skyscraper.

CHAPTER 5

Brazil: The Reign of Agribusiness

The old man has a high forehead, skin darkened by the sun, a posture bent from a lifetime working in the fields. His face is lucid, marked by a single vertical wrinkle buried deep into his right cheek like a ditch. His calloused hands are like two spades, which he waves in big circles to indicate a distant point on the horizon. 'Here, until the 1970s, it was all forest, there were trees, there were animals. It was another world. They've taken our world away.'

The man is a Guarani Indian. He's the chief of his community, the group's living memory, the one who remembers and passes on. He speaks for everybody: his extended family, who came to meet me at the entrance to the camp, is now grouped around him and listening attentively. Sitting on a wooden bench and some old plastic chairs well past their best, are about ten children, a few other men, and some women with square faces and sweet smiles slightly tainted by the hardships of life. They all live in a couple of wooden shacks in the back. A boy with protruding cheekbones and brilliant white teeth is reading a magazine, engrossed. On the cover is another Guarani; it looks like an image reflected in a mirror. A baby girl is crying: she's just fallen and her forehead is plastered with mud. A woman cleans it with a cloth. The girl keeps crying. The old man talks and tells. Beside him, an even older man is listening to him without moving. He doesn't speak Portuguese, but he gets the drift of the conversation. Every now and then he shakes himself from his apparent torpor and says something to the teller, as if imploring him to add some detail or other, to complete a line of thinking. Staring directly at me, the old man resumes his story of an existence marked by torment and injustice. 'They took our land away. And now we are here, with nothing in our hands, in what used to be our home.'

Mato Grosso do Sul, on Brazil's western extremity, is a frontier region near the border with Paraguay. The landscape is green but flat: there are no trees. Only plantations that extend as far as the eye can see. Once this was *cerrado*, a tropical environment similar to the savanna, an ecosystem with an extremely high degree of biodiversity. Today it is mostly soya cultivations. The Mato Grosso do Sul, along with its twin state further north (the Mato Grosso), Paraguay, a part of Bolivia, and East Argentina, together form the so-called 'united republic of soya' – a stretch of millions of hectares given over to the cultivation of the 'little miracle plant' whose seeds are used all over the world as animal feed, but also as an oil in many human cultures. Brazil is the world's second-largest exporter of soya. Its soya fields were created in recent decades during a westward race that has echoes of the North American Far West.

White colonists armed with tractors and chainsaws cut down the trees, occupied the land, and tilled the fields. They came from the rich states of the south of Brazil. They came with their families to create plantations. And they chased away those who were already there. 'Today, most of the land is in their hands. They arrived one day with a piece of paper that said the land belonged to them, and they told us to go away. We don't have any certificates. We didn't buy this land. We were just born on it. We are part of it. For us this land is our mother, our father. The land is everything. It gives us food and it gives us life,' says the old man, staring right into my eyes and moving his hands towards the horizon to indicate the vastness of the lands upon which his ancestors once lived, farmed and hunted without restrictions. Dispossessed of their lands, confined to barren reservations, often used as low-cost labourers, the Guarani still continue to claim – with scant chance of success – their land, which is now occupied by big landowners or *fazenderos*. Today in Mato Grosso do Sul, 11,000 Guarani live on a 3,500 hectare reserve, literally besieged by large soya plantations. Those who rebel against the situation – which the former Minister for the Environment and Brazilian Ecology leader, Marina Silva, didn't hesitate to call 'social apartheid' – are often murdered: in 2008 there were sixty murders of indigenous people in Brazil, forty-two of them from the Guarani in Mato Grosso do Sul.[1] Social disintegration has led to frequent fighting within these reserves and is the cause of one of the highest suicide rates in the world.[2]

The old man recounts the various stages of the story. His tale is a long one, typical of a culture with an oral tradition which relies on repetition so as not to forget its roots. When I ask him how long it has been like this, he takes it as a sign to reach deep into the past. He starts from the sixteenth century and the arrival of the first whites. He talks about the Jesuit missions, which enjoyed great success here up until the Suppression of the Society of Jesus. Then onto the Independence of Brazil and the War of the Triple Alliance (Brazil, Uruguay and Argentina) against Paraguay, after which the Guarani suffered much oppression due to a suspicion of connivance with the enemy. Only after a good half-hour does he get to modern times, to the mass deforestation and the landowners who finally removed them from their land. The years sometimes get a little mixed up, but the basis of his story is clear, concrete, almost tangible. All it takes is one look around to understand the true sense of his words in all their cruel reality. Barely one hundred metres away, a perfectly tilled field starts, and extends as far as the eye can see. The earth is fresh. The ultra-modern tractors are switched off. 'In a few days they will start to sow the soya,' the old man says.

The inhabitants of the camp take me to see the small plot on which they plant the little food they live on: potatoes, carrots, lettuce. In a yard there are five or six hens. They have grabbed this almost insignificant patch of land by tooth and nail. They came here at night and occupied it. Then they built the shacks and set about cultivating the land. 'We've come to take back what was ours.' The *fazendero* who has the ownership rights to this place has let them be for now, perhaps because they occupy such a tiny strip of his land. 'But we are always on alert. We know that at any moment he can send his men or the police to chase us away.' I study the old man, the extended family around him, their lifeless expressions, their miserable cultivations, and can't help thinking that theirs is a lost cause. The prevailing model is all around them: the vast plantations. They have no part to play in this model, apart from providing labour as day workers, an agricultural proletariat who no longer control their means of production. Defeat is certain and there is no appeal: this old man and his group are residuals of a world that is bound to disappear. Extensive plantation is modernity, and it will brush them away.

The 'five sisters' of soya

Mato Grosso do Sul is a laboratory for the future. It is one of the lands on which the big transnational agribusiness companies have been concentrating for more than twenty years. On the road leading from the north towards the city of Dourados, a large frontier *borgo* a hundred kilometres from the Paraguay border, the greenery of the soya fields that seem to have no end is interspersed with the enormous structures of the sector's giants: the American companies Cargill, Archer Daniels Midland (ADM), Bunge, and the French Louis Dreyfuss. The structures are stockpiling and processing plants.

These few companies, together with a handful of others, control practically the whole of the world's market for basic food products – soya, wheat, corn. They are the ones who buy the fruit of the harvests and then sell it around the world. They don't directly control the land, except where the profits to be made are extremely high. This means that they are protected from a bad year, which spells trouble not for them but for the farmers. Nonetheless, they still run the process from beginning to end, from production to marketing, thus reaping the immense returns from the sale and exportation of these products. Their transnational nature allows them to modify their supply according to economic convenience, by repeatedly exploiting the export subsidies provided by the countries from which they export and manoeuvring around the customs duties of those who import their goods. Their giant storehouses allow them to sell when prices on the international market are higher – and thereby to influence the market. What they have set up is a perfect oligarchy.

To take the soya sector alone, five big companies – Cargill, ADM, Bunge, Louis Dreyfuss and the Brazilian company Avipal – control 60 percent of the Brazilian market and 80 percent of exports to Europe. On a wider scale, Cargill and ADM together control 65 percent of the world's cereal market.[3] Other big companies, often belonging to these groups or linked to them through powerful and lucrative synergies, control the so-called inputs: fertilisers, pesticides, seeds. As the CEO of Cargill put it, 'we produce phosphorus fertilisers in Tampa, Florida. These fertilisers are used in the United States and in Argentina to grow soya. The soya is processed and transformed into feed and oil. The feed is sent to Thailand to feed chickens, which are then treated, cooked and packaged, to be sent to fridges in Japan or Europe.'[4]

One look around is enough to realise how all-pervasive these companies have become. On the main Mato Grosso do

Sul road, which connects its capital, Campo Grande, to Dourados, beside each field a sign indicates the type and variety of cultivation that's going on there: they are all genetically modified seeds and the brands are those of Syngenta or Monsanto. Following pressure from the agribusiness companies, Brazil opened its doors to genetically modified organisms,[5] which are still banned in Europe by virtue of the 'precautionary principle'.[6]

The power these transnational companies wield is enormous, their turnover astronomical, and their influence on the policies of entire states profound. In this part of the world, the *fazenderos*, who themselves enjoy a handsome income from their plantations, call the companies that buy up the soya the 'five sisters'.

The landowners and the multinationals

'The cultivators are caught in the middle of a sandwich', says Erminio Guedes dos Santos, an engineer who runs a sort of union for Dourados's agricultural producers. 'All the power is in the hands of the corporations. The farmers aren't in a position to decide the price. And they pay for this: even when prices on the world's markets are high, their profits are reduced by the so-called bottlenecks. If a few companies control both the inputs and the marketing, those involved in the production process have a low profit margin.' Erminio is of average height, jovial, about fifty, with a squint that tilts even further to the right when he laughs. When I go to meet him at the union's office, it's immediately clear he's going to be helpful. As soon as I walk into the office, a small room with one computer and a wooden table piled with documents in no apparent order, and before I've had a chance to introduce myself or explain the reason for my visit, he puts on his jacket, gives me a slap on the back, and says: 'It's lunchtime. Let's go to the fair. We can talk there while we eat.' The 'fair' is a big agricultural exhibition organised every year in Dourados. It's held on uncultivated land at the entrance to the city, a couple of hundred metres from the Cargill plant, which greets visitors with imposing silos and large signs in block letters which are much bigger than the welcome signs put up by the municipality. Between the warehouses of the exhibition there are stands selling the very latest tractor models. Others are displaying fertilisers, or machines for sowing and irrigation.

There's also a simple restaurant, with plastic seats and tables, a big umbrella to give shade from the sun, and generous helpings of tasty-looking meat. As we're waiting for our lunch, Erminio fills me in on his work, which seems like a very desperate endeavour. 'We're trying to break the monopoly that these groups have. We're trying to build storage structures which can give us greater autonomy. But often the multinationals are in league with the big *fazenderos*, to whom they offer better prices in a deliberate attempt to break the farmers' united front. As a result, the small farmer has no future and eventually ends up selling his plot to the big boys.'

Perhaps the best example in Brazil of the big *fazendero* is Blairo Maggi, better known as *o rei da soia*. The owner of over 300,000 hectares of land, mostly used for soya, in 2003 he was elected Governor of Mato Grosso, the nerve centre of his activity. Awarded the 'golden chainsaw' by Greenpeace for his contribution to the deforestation of his state and the advancement of the soya frontier from the *cerrado* towards the Amazon rainforest, Maggi won the election precisely because he furthered the cause of big agrarian business, which is based on the landed estate system.

'This', continues Erminio, tucking in to a succulent beef steak that has found its way to the table, 'is one of Brazil's main vices: the concentration of land in the hands of a few. In the soya-growing region here in Mato Grosso do Sul, in Mato Grosso, in the state of Rondônia and as far as Santarém, in

Pará in the Amazon forest, there is a density of landed estates – lands that exceed a thousand hectares – which is among the highest in the world.'[7]

Once we've finished lunch we go for a stroll around the stands. There's a video demonstrating the performance of a machine for spraying fertiliser. Some children are having fun climbing on a tractor. We decide to meet again that evening to continue our conversation. After sunset, the place is a lot more crowded: swarms of kids have come to hang around, families with their youngsters, farmers with their bellies hanging out, gobbling huge plates of meat and washing it all down with litres of *cachaça*, the strong and sweet Brazilian liqueur. The Guarani are there too, looking a little lost as they wander around half-heartedly trying to sell small handicraft products. It's all very much indicative of Dourados itself: a borgo that was born on the wave of the Brazilian agricultural miracle, in a frontier region, and that has grown in a hurry and without the necessary social safety nets. On the streets of the town can be seen the latest SUVs and brand new motorbikes. The Toyota dealer's office is always full. The shops are stacked with pricey electrical goods. Meanwhile, on the side of the streets, the few citizens with darker skin travel on foot or cling to battered bicycles. Class distinctions here are clear and unabashedly flaunted, and follow well-defined ethnic lines. The whites are the bosses, they have come from elsewhere and have taken public power by force and connivance, and now they run what used to belong to others. The colonisation is complete. The facts on the ground speak for themselves: those who have always lived here seem resigned to scrapping for the crumbs and paltry leftovers of a party that is going on at their expense. They live on the fringes, on the little or nothing that has been left to them, and take refuge in alcoholism or slide into depression. They are defeated, and no longer have the strength to get back on their feet. In the words of Anastácio

Peralta, a Guarani who has studied anthropology and shows me around the camps, 'once there was no Brazil, no Bolivia, no Argentina. It was all our land. They took it away from us, and we let them, we didn't fight hard enough. It's not easy to live with this sense of defeat.'

'Somebody's got to do the dirty work'

'Welcome', says Celso Dal Lago as he shakes my hand. An imposing man, as sturdy as a tree, with cerulean eyes, a small mouth, and thin hair that can just about be seen under the cowboy hat that seems to be the trademark of any self-respecting landowner in these parts. Celso is a *fazendero*. Erminio introduces him to me at the fair, explaining the work I'm doing, and he willingly agrees to show me around his land. He suggests seven o'clock the next morning, perhaps to show me that even estate owners work hard and sleep little. At seven on the button the next morning he's at my hotel to pick me up in his car, a big white jeep which he then proceeds to race at high speed through the still-abandoned streets of Dourados. We drive for about half an hour, and he tells me about how he came to Mato Grosso do Sul. His family emigrated to Brazil from Veneto. Initially they settled in Rio Grande do Sul, the southern agricultural state where most Italian emigrants landed at the turn of the twentieth century. Then his father got married and decided to take advantage of the opportunities presented by the 'virgin lands of the West'. He uses this exact expression, which sounds like something right out of a saga on the gold rush to the Klondike. 'He came to Dourados in the fifties, when there was nothing here. He built an empire with his bare hands.' 'And here it is,' he says, turning right and onto a dirt road, 'we've just come on to our land.' There are no fences and no signs. Just hectare upon hectare of sugarcane. We drive through it in the jeep, the green cane rising to two metres in height. It completely covers the horizon, making it impossible to see what lies beyond. We drive for another quarter of an hour without seeing a soul. The property seems endless. Then Celso turns right again and makes for a field where a massive machine is smashing its way through the clods, a sort of giant metal elephant leaving mountains of cane in its wake in preparation for further planting. 'The harvest is almost ready there, and here we're starting to sow.'

We continue to talk as we walk by the field. A group of Guarani in long-sleeved shirts and rubber boots are in the process of sowing seeds, neatly lining the cut cane in little ditches. They look tired. They wave at the boss, and he waves back. I decide to needle him a little. I tell him that some groups and organisations insist that the land we are on belongs to the indigenous tribes. He looks straight at me without batting an eye, then says: 'If you look at history, you'll find that all of Latin America once belonged to the indigenous tribes. The whole of Brazil was an indigenous state. But you have to take into consideration that since then development has taken place. Land has been tilled. Fields have been cultivated. Because of our hard labour the country has entered into the global system, and its development is benefitting everyone, even the indigenous tribes. Those who say the land should be given back to the indios have their head in the clouds: that's a primitive and nostalgic mentality. They'd like to go back to the seventeenth century, and see the indigenous tribes in their primitive state. But look at them there in the fields: they're working, earning, they're integrated into a productive system.'

I answer that working in a sugarcane field is backbreaking, and some would consider it a form of slavery. Celso isn't the slightest bit rattled: 'there's all this talk about this being backbreaking work', he answers. 'Of course it's backbreaking, but it's no worse than that of a miner going down into a mine to extract coal. Everybody has got their own economic potential: people earn according to their culture and what service they provide. Somebody has to work. Otherwise, if we all laze about in air-conditioned rooms, there'll be no more wheat, no more sugarcane, no meat, no nothing. We wouldn't even have a TV if nobody did the manual labour. It boils down to this: if we want the TV, the air conditioning, somebody's got to do the dirty work.'

Dal Lago doesn't mince his words. Nor does he hide behind the standard politically correct expressions. He makes no attempt to deny the inequality present in work relations or, for that matter, throughout the entire production system. In fact, he practically defends it as a good thing. Finding oneself among the winners – those who have the TVs and the air conditioning – is a sign of success, of a battle strenuously fought, of a colonisation that allowed families of emigrants who had nothing to build authentic agrarian empires. I'm struck by the thought that such a conversation would be impossible, deemed almost criminal, in a Europe imbued with the enlightenment and egalitarianism that hides its exploitative practices behind hypocritical expressions such as 'shared responsibility' and 'development participation'. The world is a lot clearer here. It's black and white. The *fazendero* commands, and the Guarani or farm workers slave day-by-day for a morsel of bread. At one stage, Celso confesses to me that he would gladly do without this army of beggars. 'I have to take on a certain number to satisfy the agreement I made with the local government. But the land here is flat: all the harvesting and sowing could be done by machines.'

Cohabitation between these two worlds is difficult. The Guarani hate the *fazenderos*; the latter, for their part, don't hide their dislike for the former, who they consider indolent, underdeveloped. Racism pervades the air, even if the target of the landowners' wrath isn't the indigenous population as much as the organisations – such as the Conselho Indigenista Missionário (CIMI) or the Fundaçao Nacional do Indio

(FUNAI) – who fight at state and federal level for a recognition of their rights. These are the 'nostalgic' dreamers Dal Lago was talking about. They are the real enemies. His words reveal that he considers them to be traitors, because they refuse the progress that the landowners are convinced they have brought. The era of the conquest of the West is still very much present in the landowners' minds: the colonisers cannot abide that a handful of whites, most of whom have grown up wrapped in cotton wool on the coast and have never even smelt the land, should come and teach them what to do. This is why they flaunt their power, using it almost as a status symbol. When, on the way back to Dourados, we pull up to a police car and I go to put on my seatbelt, a more relaxed Dal Lago makes a sign that I shouldn't bother. He says, looking at me from under his cowboy hat: 'No need for that. We're in charge here, not them.'

Celso speeds past field after field before turning in towards a small hut. This is the *fazenda* office: three rooms, a sofa, a couple of desks, a computer, little else. The walls are bare, the floors tiled. No trace of luxury or exuberant wealth. In comparison with the large agricultural properties in Rio Grande do Sul or São Paulo state, where colonisation began earlier, this area doesn't have big imposing mansions. There are no servants and waiters in full livery, which is what I have been expecting. This is the frontier: the *fazenderos* live in the city, and when they do stay out in the country they sleep in their clothes on a sofa or even on the floor. This hut is the sign of a wealth recently obtained, but which has not yet wiped out the memory of a peasant past. We leave the office and stop at a fence. Dal Lago tells me that he has changed his crop. He used to produce soya, like everybody else in Dourados. He has diversified into sugarcane, which now covers a large part of his extensive land. 'I started a few years ago. The sugarcane you see here is part of a project to produce three million tons per season, which can produce around six million litres of ethanol and 135,000 tons of sugar. All of this produce, especially the ethanol, is initially destined for the internal market, but our main objective is to produce ethanol for exportation, especially to Asian countries such as China and Japan.'

Dal Lago appears to be fully immersed in the state's new trend, which is to produce sugarcane for agrofuels. The Mato Grosso do Sul is the last frontier for producing ethanol from sugarcane – traditionally grown in the state of São Paulo – and for diesel extracted from soya. According to Conab, a Brazilian government agency that is part of the Ministry for Agriculture, the 2007–8 harvest saw an increase of 51,000 hectares of sugarcane grown in the state, or 32 percent more than the previous year. In August 2008, the state's Governor, André Puccinelli, predicted that 'in the next seven years Mato Grosso do Sul will become the world's leading producer of ethanol'.[8] Dal Lago tells me that many of his colleagues and friends have gone into sugarcane production. 'It's a very promising sector.' I ask him who he sells his produce to. He says that he would like to buy shares in a refinery they are building nearby, but for now he is selling 'to the usual five sisters'. Cargill, ADM, and Bunge have been particularly active in the new fuel business, buying shares in refineries, and not only in Mato Grosso do Sul. Through some of their subsidiaries, they have also bought up tracts of land to use directly for biofuel production. 'Brazil is now part of a global context and these large marketing companies are also looking to get into production. This is a new trend: previously they limited themselves to buying the goods,' he points out. Even in the Brazil of the *fazenderos* land grabbing is silently underway, a little less brazenly than in Africa, but just as worryingly. So much so that in August 2010 the federal government was obliged to impose a limit of 5,000 hectares on land acquisitions by foreigners. According to the Instituto Nacional de Colonização e Reforma Agrária (INCRA), a public agency that keeps a register of agricultural land, 11.7 percent of the land in Mato Grosso do Sul is already in foreign hands, and the primary goal of these groups is to produce agrofuels for exportation.

The new ethanol civilisation

'I think that it's an irreversible trend. Big business is investing in ethanol because this is the fuel of the future.' Roberto Rodrigues is a man with a broad perspective, who likes to think big and make long-term predictions. He was the Minister for Agriculture during Luis Inácio 'Lula' da Silva's first mandate, and is considered the undisputed champion of the pro-ethanol lobby. Rodrigues was the brains behind the massive public relations operation in favour of agrofuels launched by the Brazilian government and personified by Lula himself, who on many occasions at international meetings defended 'the advantages for the reduction of greenhouse gases', and rejected as non-existent any link between the rise in ethanol consumption and the increase in food prices.

Brazil has a long history of agrofuel production. It began to produce them on a large scale as far back as the mid 1970s with the Proálcool programme, launched during the era of the military dictatorship in response to the rise in petrol prices and the fall in the value of sugar on the international markets.[9] Through a policy of subsidies and negative-interest loans, the military in power in Brasilia were trying to kill two birds with one stone: to resolve the energy problem and overcome the social and economic crisis caused by a reduction in the value of what was Brazil's biggest export. In doing so, they created a new industry. Dozens of refineries were built, and a lot more land was given over to the cultivation of sugarcane. By 1986, 90 percent of cars sold ran on ethanol. Then came the cold shower. The fall in petrol prices put a stop to the party: by the end of the 1990s nobody in Brazil was producing ethanol any more, and the country even started importing it from the United States. The number of cars that used agrofuels fell to a paltry 1 percent. Fuel from sugarcane seemed to all intents and purposes a closed chapter. Over the past ten years, however, two new elements have contributed to a relaunching of the project: on the one hand there was the soaring price of crude oil, and on the other the development of flex-fuel technology, which allows consumers to put both ethanol and petrol into the same tank, thus giving them a choice at the pumps. In the space of a few years ethanol production was back up and running, reaching twenty-five billion litres in 2009.

Today, Brazil is the world's second-biggest ethanol producer after the United States, where the industry's success is primarily due to the public subsidies. In Brazil, by contrast, the business is turning a profit by itself, given that production costs are lower and because the energy return is much higher from sugarcane than from corn. The food-fuel debate so contentious in the United States is less heated in Brazil: the amount of land on which sugarcane is grown is seven million hectares, which is equally divided between ethanol and sugar production. This means that cultivation for agrofuels represents approximately 5 percent of the 63 million hectares of land being cultivated in the country, and 1 percent of the land which is suitable for cultivation. These figures go a long way to explaining why the business has started to attract the attention not only of the traditional 'sugar barons' – the big families that have always controlled the sector – but also of international companies, who are interested in producing in Brazil especially in light of the expansion of the lucrative export market. The increase in demand from the Asian countries, and the need for Europe to meet its declared objective of replacing 10 percent of its petrol use with alternative renewable sources of energy by 2020,[10] are also incentives for large-scale investment to increase the production and export of fuel 'made in Brazil'. The same is true for the United States which has, as mentioned in the previous chapter, set itself similar targets for an increase in the use of biofuels.

Brazil and the United States are on the same side in the planetary battle to promote agrofuels. In March 2007 an 'alliance for ethanol' between the two states was cemented by George W. Bush and Lula amid handshakes and hugs. The 'alliance' makes provision for the sharing of technology and capital to produce ethanol in Central America, in a group of countries linked to the United States by the CAFTA[11] free trade agreement.

Behind this agreement – and behind Bush's repeated statements in favour of ethanol, from his 2006 State of the Union speech to the approval of legislation soon after for an increase in the consumption of renewable energy – there is a powerful pressure group that moves between Brazil and the United States and has continental aspirations: the Interamerican Ethanol Commission, whose declared objective is 'to convince the governments of the western hemisphere to increase their use of agrofuels'. The founders of this commission are none other than Roberto Rodrigues and Jeb Bush – the former Governor of Florida and younger brother of the former US President. It's no secret that it was the Interamerican Ethanol Commission that brought about the meetings, the signing of the agreement, and the handshake between Bush and Lula. Neither is it a secret that behind this alliance lies the desire to become independent from other oil-producing countries and to put in place a new energy balance in the world.

Roberto Rodrigues is the man to meet to understand this mechanism. 'All we did was talk to our respective Presidents and give them some advice,' he says dismissively. I'm meeting him early one morning at the University of São Paulo, where he runs a research programme on agrofuels. It's 7.30 a.m.;

when I called him the day before he told me to be in his office at that time. 'If it's not too early for you,' he added with a cordial tone, from which I understood that there was no alternative. The building is deserted. The man at reception, his eyes still heavy from sleep, has my name written on a little slip of paper. He greets me – *Bom dia* – and hands me a pass. I go up the stairs and arrive at a little room, where I find one small table, two seats, and a secretary hard at work despite the early hour. 'This way please, Professor Rodrigues is expecting you,' says the girl, opening the door to a much bigger room, lit by large windows, and with a long desk at the end, a full book-case, and walls covered with photos, diplomas, awards, honorary degrees and so on. Rodrigues is short, with a round face and slightly sunken eyes with which he examines me carefully. He is about sixty years old. The photos behind his desk show a series of children and grandchildren. He comes to meet me with a smile. He's dressed in a long-sleeved shirt and tie, and on the pocket of his shirt is written, in small but legible letters, his initials: R.R. He apologises for the early hour of our appointment. 'But I'm leaving for a long weekend with my family at my country house.'

Still a little hazy from the dawn start, I start asking him about the commission of which he is the co-founder. But he is anxious to get straight to it, answering a question I hadn't asked him yet even though it is on everybody's lips: 'This dispute between food and fuel is a red herring. Biofuel is totally different to food produce. It needs a lot more sun. It doesn't grow in the same environment.'

'That', I answer, 'may be valid for sugarcane, but not for corn.' 'I've tried to explain to our American friends that corn isn't suitable for producing ethanol, but they have a big internal problem and for the moment they cannot change their policy.' The 'big internal problem' is obviously the lobby by the Midwest farmers, who produce ethanol and survive largely through federal subsidies for distribution. Rodrigues is a bona fide prophet of agrofuels; he considers himself a visionary whose ideas and plans are destined to shape the future of the entire planet. 'Civilisation at present is like a giant with clay feet,' he says emphatically. 'It is based on an energy source that is destined to end: fossil fuels. None of this makes sense.'

'I believe', Rodrigues continues, staring directly at me with his sunken eyes, 'that a new civilisation is imminent, and that its driving force will be agrofuels.' His idea is that renewable energies, particularly those created from grown produce, represent the fulcrum of an epochal geopolitical change, for which Brazil must act as promoter. Moving his hands in opposite directions, almost as if he is fiddling with a Rubik's cube, he fills me in on the details of his vision for the future. 'Biofuels and agro energy will develop between the Tropic of Cancer and the Tropic of Capricorn, a strip that covers all of Latin America, all of sub-Saharan Africa and a large part of the poorer regions in Asia. What is set to change is the world agricultural paradigm. But world geopolitics will also change, because these tropical countries are poorer, with less work and less wealth. Between the two tropics we have ample land, water, sun and labour. What we don't have is capital. The capital will come from the north, where most of the energy will be consumed.' According to Rodrigues' vision, the states in the north must stop buying petroleum at exorbitant prices from countries that are often unstable and unreliable, and start to invest directly in the production of agrofuels – which are 'less polluting, cheaper and, above all, inexhaustible' – in countries in the southern part of the world.

The plan hides one necessity, which the former minister immediately reveals. 'I believe that agrofuels will be the most important commodities of the twenty-first century. But for this to happen they must expand, diversify, and be produced in many parts of the world, just like petroleum.'

The objective Brazil has set for itself is precisely this: to ensure that ethanol becomes a commodity, a good whose value is negotiated on international markets. To realise that goal, the market must be broadened, not just for consumers but also for suppliers, who cannot be too restricted. From this stems the Bush-Lula pact for production in Central America and the various initiatives launched in sub-Saharan Africa, in the zone 'that spans from the Tropic of Cancer and the Tropic of Capricorn'. From this stems the idea of a new 'agricultural paradigm'. And from this also comes the necessity to open the Brazilian ethanol market to the transnational agribusiness and petroleum companies.

The project is ambitious but not totally impracticable. The United States and the European Union have given themselves binding targets for short-term increases in the use of agrofuels. Petroleum is running out and is too concentrated in unstable areas of the world run by unreliable governments. The plan proposed by the former minister could represent a viable alternative. But it doesn't take into account one element: Brazil is as big as a continent, has land aplenty and can easily afford to allot a portion of it to fuel production. Not all of the countries positioned between the Tropics of Cancer and Capricorn – in fact, none of them, except perhaps the Democratic Republic of Congo, which is covered in forest and practically devoid of infrastructure – present the same characteristics. In this region, the dispute between food and fuel is not a 'red herring'. It personally effects millions of people who live and work in the fields and may have to give up their culture and change their habits overnight to facilitate the birth of this 'new civilisation' – from which it is highly unlikely that they will be among the first to benefit.

'The diabolical alliance of big business'
João Pedro Stedile is a tall man, with a white beard, sky-blue eyes and a deep, cavernous voice that every now and then

explodes into a piercing laugh. He is the spokesman for one of the most famous social movements in the world – the Movimento dos Trabalhadores Rurais Sem Terra, or Movement of Landless Workers (MST) – responsible for great struggles for agrarian reform and memorable occupations of land, and consistently at the forefront in the fight against the *fazenderos* and agribusiness companies. Stedile himself has declared that since its birth in 1984 the movement has liberated fourteen million hectares and helped 370,000 families to enforce their right to their land.

I go to meet him at the Movement's São Paulo office, a slightly derelict detached house near the city centre. Once inside I am taken to a small waiting room, with two little sofas, a few chairs, and a crumbling wall adorned with yellowing posters. Just outside there is a desk that functions as a reception area, where a phone rings incessantly. A lone girl is in charge of operating the switchboard: every time she ends one call she immediately finds another one waiting. I watch as she answers and then hangs up, hangs up and then answers, and think back to a couple of days previously, when I had called from Rome to talk to the person responsible for international relations to set up a meeting with Stedile. I had spent a full hour dialling the number, which was constantly engaged, before finally managing to get through. Having cursed her on that Roman afternoon, I now watch the receptionist with a mixture of admiration and sympathy: she's working like a machine, putting calls through to various extensions and providing information herself whenever she can. I almost nod off to sleep sitting there, listening as she answers with remarkable cordiality. Then, after an hour has passed, two members of the movement arrive to tell me that we have to go somewhere else. 'O *companheiro* João Pedro has just finished a meeting and is waiting for you, but not here. We're going to him.' I get into a van with them. From my seat in the back I can't see where we are going. The van speeds along and after about twenty minutes we arrive at what looks like a run-down school. The building has two floors and a small garden. On the ground floor there's a long room with a large rough wooden table. Above this room there are two more, one for meetings and another for the courses the movement organises for its affiliates. In one of these rooms – chairs stacked against the walls, a blackboard still covered in writing, and the inevitable Brazilian flag with its inscription *Ordem e Progresso* – Stedile is waiting for me. He greets me with a warm hug, maybe because I have been recommended to him by a mutual friend, who is also the unofficial representative of Sem Terra in Italy. He apologises for the delay – it's two hours after the time we were supposed to meet. 'There was a meeting that ran on a bit. I hope I haven't created any problems for you.' I smile and tell him that I am happy to see him. The truth is I am totally exhausted, having arrived that morning from Italy and then spent the entire day travelling around São Paulo: it's now nine in the evening – or one in the morning in Italian time.

I muster the energy to start the interview. Stedile is cheerful, extroverted. It's clear that he likes to talk. He starts telling me about his relationship with Italy. His family is also originally from the Veneto region, and he too is a product of the mass emigration that took place at the turn of the twentieth century. He tells me that he has even gone to visit the town where his grandparents came from, and met some distant relatives. He has been to Italy many times, but 'unfortunately I don't speak your language, although I do understand it'. Stedile is often on the move: he and the other leaders of Sem Terra are also part of Via Campesina, the group of farm associations that continue to fight for the survival of small-scale sustainable agriculture. They meet at the organisation's big summits and at various meetings on food sovereignty, where they integrate their own struggle with that of small farmers from West

Africa, Southeast Asia and Central America. Sem Terra adopts basically the same general position as Via Campesina. They regard the new trend for biofuels as 'another step towards driving small farmers from their land'.

'So you are against agrofuels?' I ask him point-blank. 'We are not necessarily against agrofuels *per se*. We think petroleum is a terrible thing, and we believe that a review of the present system is badly needed: it's a system based on individual transport with an absurd waste of energy and produces a frighteningly large amount of greenhouse gases and other forms of pollution. As for agrofuels, we are against the way in which they are being developed. Here in Brazil we are witnessing the creation of a diabolical alliance that unites three big sectors of international capital: the oil companies, the transnational companies that control agricultural commerce and genetically modified seeds, and the car manufacturers.'

Stedile doesn't speak in slogans. He provides information and numbers. By way of his network of militants and the many academics close to the movement he has been able to draw up a detailed map of the new investments in the sector. 'The March 2007 agreement was a green light for the safe entry of international capital into Brazil. More than fourteen billion dollars in investment came this way. They are also building two alcohol ducts, one from Cuiabá to Paranaguá, another from Goriás to Santos. Along these alcohol ducts they are already building seventy-seven new ethanol factories. A great number of these factories are owned by international businesses.'

Listening to this organiser of a grassroots movement I see him as the counterpart of Roberto Rodrigues. At times Stedile uses the same words as the former Minister for Agriculture, but with the opposite meaning. The project for the future elaborated by the Interamerican Ethanol Commission is, in his view, the worst thing that could happen to humanity:

'There's a big plan being put in place to produce agrofuels not just in Brazil but throughout the global south, where the best conditions exist, because there is a greater degree of solar energy and a lot of available land. All this will do is provoke the spreading of monoculture plantations, run by big business, where goods destined for food consumption will be redirected in order to produce fuel. They want to export to Africa or to South Asia a model that is already causing untold damage in Brazil.'

I repeat the argument made by Rodrigues and the entire ethanol-producing industry: 'In your country there is no real dispute between food and fuel. The area used to grow sugarcane for ethanol represents only 5 percent of the total.' This causes a flicker in Stedile's azure eyes. I realise he is surprised, but it's hard to decipher what he's thinking: I can't tell if he's annoyed at the impertinent comment, or grateful for the assist that will allow him to introduce a subject close to his heart. After a few seconds of reflection, he formulates his answer: 'What you have said is not altogether true. The area where sugarcane is being grown is moving towards the centre of the country, where the most fertile land can be found. The cane is already displacing the cultivation of beans, corn, as well as pastures for the rearing of animals for dairy and meat. This is going to cause a lot of problems for food production in Brazil. Without taking into account another aspect: in agriculture, when a product brings a higher rate of profit, all other food prices rise. Given that ethanol has caused the average profits in agriculture to rise, all the other agricultural products have risen. This is the most perverse effect, from an economic perspective, arising from what's happening in Brazil. The price of land has risen, the prices of agricultural products have risen, and so the average level of prices has been raised by ethanol.'

I listen to Stedile and think again about Rodrigues. The two are polar opposites, from every point of view. Physically, one is tall and strong; the other is short and a little obese. At a formal level, one welcomes you late in the evening, two hours late, in a room full of stacked chairs; the other sees you at precisely the agreed time, at dawn, in his office, which is adorned with plaudits. Their experiences, their lifestyles, their ideas, are totally opposed. One has spent his life organising grassroots battles, creating a movement whose most effective weapon is land occupation and whose main demand is for agrarian reform; the other represents big business investing in agriculture. They are the most complete expressions of opposite environments, which don't communicate with each other and rarely intersect. They have two different models of reference, two visions of the world, and therefore two plans for the future of Brazil that offer no possibility of synthesis. They represent two groups, one powerful and rich, the other more numerous. On one side, the agribusiness multinationals, the investors I met in Geneva, the *fazenderos* of Mato Grosso do Sul – people who don't always have the same interests but are equally committed to 'economies of scale', increasing productivity, the conquering of foreign markets; on the other side, the small farmers like those whose performance I watched at the FAO summit, who want to continue to cultivate their land without being squashed by the representatives of the first group.

Stedile is the Brazilian counterpart of Henry Saragih: tenacious, combative, sure of his ideas. From his words – and from the words I have exchanged with other organisers and militants in São Paulo or Mato Grosso do Sul – I get an impression which is clear, sure, indelible. In contrast to the Guarani Indians, who seem to have interjected their condition as the defeated, the MST representatives have the strength and the desire to fight. They have a clear model of society. Movements such as Sem Terra – and many others around the world, from the Network of Farmers' and Agricultural Producers'

Organisations of West Africa (ROPPA) to Saragih's Indonesia Peasant Union – try to convey to small farmers the need to remain on the land, to resist the pressure from the large transnational companies and the new investors in the agricultural sector. By creating consortiums, they try to resist the immense power of men like Rodrigues and other defenders of the principal facets of agribusiness: extensive monoculture plantations, commercial agriculture, a focus on exports. Theirs is a difficult battle, and destined to become even harder over the coming years. A battle in which no compromise will likely be possible. The two groups represented by Stedile and Rodrigues are destined to clash more often given that, while belonging to different universes, they live in the same world and are competing for a common resource – the land – which is increasingly scarce and becoming ever more valuable. As I reflect on my conversations with Stedile and Rodrigues and on their respective arguments, I come to the conclusion that the situation in Brazil prefigures what is happening and will happen increasingly often throughout the world over the coming years. Having an enormous concentration of land ownership and having experienced an extraordinary level of penetration by agrofuel multinationals, Brazil has been a hotbed for movements demanding agrarian reform and a flashpoint for conflict over land. Such conflicts are bound to be extended globally, and to lead to increasingly fraught clashes between the representatives of small farmers and those of big business. The result of these clashes will almost certainly determine the kind of planet we will be living on over the course of the twenty-first century.

CHAPTER 6

Tanzania: The Frontier for Biofuels

Row upon row, long and orderly, extending endlessly. The plantation covers the entire plain, sloping up the hills, sprawling beyond the horizon. Eight thousand hectares, or the equivalent of twelve thousand football fields. There are no fences, only white signs, spread out at intervals, with red writing: *No Entry*. The plantation has only one crop: a small plant less than a metre high, with large leaves attached to a stem well-rooted in the earth. The pale green leaves don't look very healthy. But that is of no importance. They'll soon be cut, and their stems pulled up in order to collect the seeds, the precious part of this plant whose name the peasants of the area now know only too well: jatropha. Capable of growing in the most impervious of environments, even in the total absence of water, this crop is considered by many the fuel of the future: oil can be extracted from its seed and used for motor fuel.

But the surrounding territory here is neither impervious nor dry. This is the Kisarawe district, approximately seventy kilometres from Dar es Salaam, Tanzania's political and economic capital. On the rich green hills surrounding the plantation, manioca and potato crops are grown. The dirt roads are lined with trees and plants of all kinds: banana trees with their customary purple flowers and lopsided green canopy, very tall coconut trees, avocado trees bursting with fruit, enormous mango trees standing out against the sky. The environment is bountiful, the earth red and shining. On the roads can be seen trucks with casks of water and men on bicycles laden with coal, the main form of energy in an area that has no electricity. The black lumps are tied to the back of the bikes in handcrafted sacks made from woven palm leaves. Stacked to the hilt, as high as three metres, from afar it looks like a series of mobile towers bouncing on two wheels. The cyclists pedal for all they're worth, zigzagging to avoid the puddles. The path is muddy. It rained only yesterday. In the fields, the peasants are at work. Men and women working their bones off among the clods. They swing their hoes, dig and then sow the seeds. This is subsistence agriculture: they consume a part of their produce themselves, and the rest is sold around the region.

The village of Muhaga is a collection of about a hundred little wooden huts dispersed throughout the fields. There's a plot of uncultivated land, used by the children to play football on, with goalposts made from two truck tyres stuck in the ground. To one side, a row of communal toilets. In a slightly larger clearing, under the shade of trees, there is a more solid brick building with blue walls: the school, built thanks to an aid programme financed by a cooperation agency. This is where the villagers greet me. 'Karibu,' welcome, they all chime in Kiswahili. There are ten of them. The chief is there, with four other men and five women of differing ages. One of the women is very old, her face suspended in an absent gaze; her large yellow tunic has a map of Africa printed on it. Her face is a clump of wrinkles, her chin sticking out. It looks like she is sleeping. A man beside her is shaking a bunch of keys. I wonder what they are for; there are no cars about and the huts have no locks. A man in his early thirties is staring at me and smiling. He nods his head to get my attention, then searches his pocket and pulls out a round, green fruit, not much bigger than a marble. He peels it, and out comes a dry brown nut. 'This is the jatropha seed. This is what they are growing on what used to be our land.'

After the introductions, Athumani Mkambala, the village chief, begins to speak. He's about fifty, short, dressed in work clothes: trousers that look a bit too big for him, a white and blue T-shirt, a pair of shoes without laces. His face is tiny and his neck seems to go on forever. He actually looks a bit like a turtle, even more so every time he laughs and reveals his teeth right back to his gums. Athumani has just shown me around the plantation. He has taken me to the top of a hill where the best photos could be taken. He has even accompanied me to the gates of the big factory when I was trying to meet some-body from the company that farms the jatropha – a pathetic scene in which I pretended, on advice from Athumani, to be a friend of one of the villagers I had met in Dar es Salaam, and was just curious to see the cultivation. 'If you say you are a journalist, they'll send you away immediately.' But they gave me my marching orders within three minutes anyway. 'Nobody here today. Come back tomorrow,' says the security guard, not believing for a minute the story of the tourist wandering around the Tanzanian countryside.

Nobody said a word, however, when we roamed freely through the plantation, armed with notebook and camera. The land was open and unprotected, apart from the *No Entry* signs that we belligerently ignored. Perhaps the reason is that it's virtually impossible to fence in 8,000 hectares of land. Throughout our tour, which lasted about an hour, Athumani pointed out particular places, and suggested good spots for taking photos. He provided me with a number of technical details on the land and on the plant growing there, but refused to answer my insistent questions about how much land had been expropriated, or how, when and why it had happened. At first he was just evasive, before explicitly cutting this particu-lar conversation short: 'Now we look. There will be time later to discuss such things.' And so I stopped asking, and concen-trated instead on studying the rows of jatropha, the water pump, the arrow indicating a warehouse 1.5 kilometres away. I kept looking at the enormous stretch of pallid little plants, and formulating the questions I wanted to ask Athumani that would have to wait for the 'time later'.

Once back at the village, we go straight to the school. Some of the meeting's participants are already there. Others arrive a few minutes later. As soon as I enter the building, I realise why Athumani has been so reticent: the village chief wants to talk in the presence of his community. He wants the experience to be a shared one. He doesn't want it to seem like he has spoken on his own to the *mzungo* journalist, the white man who has come from Europe. Sitting at his desk surrounded by his community, Athumani clearly feels more at ease, and officially opens the meeting. He tells me about the foreigners' arrival and how they started to grow the plant which is now dominating the countryside. He speaks slowly, trying to remember every detail. Every so often someone else intervenes to remind him of a specific fact, or something he hasn't yet mentioned. The discussion gradually becomes more choral, or as choral as it can be considering that every phrase must be translated for me from Kiswahili to English.

From the version told by Athumani and the others, the story that emerges is one of dispossession by means of trickery, of promises made but not kept, of corruption by public powers at various levels. It all started in 2006. A parliamentarian from the Kisarawe district came to Muhaga. He said there was an investor interested in growing jatropha. He asked the village to give up a part of its land and hand it over to the businessman. 'This is a unique development opportunity. The foreign company will build a new school, a hospital, a water pump, roads. It will give compensation money to all of the families. And it will create new jobs.' The village assembly came together. Many of them were opposed. The parliamentarian came back. He said that the investor was interested in an area that included land belonging to eleven villages, and that the other ten villages had already accepted.

'He told us that we were the only ones left. At the end of 2008, we gave our consent. Then we discovered that the parliamentarian had used the same trick with all eleven villages.'

More than two years later, the Muhaga villagers still have the same dirt roads, no hospital, the same single-roomed classroom, and no water pump for running water. Still no sign of any compensation money either. 'Only two families have received any kind of indemnity,' says Athumani. The only promise that was kept was the one about jobs: a couple of hundred people from various villages are employed on the plantations, with contracts of 108,000 shillings a month (about 54 euros). The pay is higher than the minimum wage set by the Tanzanian government, but conditions are very difficult. 'We work from 7.30 to 5.30,' says the man who has shown me the seed, and who has worked there for about a year. 'They give us an hour's break for lunch, which we bring from home. We're constantly under the sun. There are no toilets. We spray pesticides without any protection for our noses. The bosses of the company are not too interested in our health.'

The company in question is Sun Biofuels, a British firm that entered the biofuel business in East Africa a few years ago. As well as this concession in Tanzania it has another in Mozambique and a small one in Ethiopia that it doesn't use for production but for conducting experiments. In Kisarawe, it has obtained its 8,000 hectares on a ninety-nine year lease. It has asked for 18,000 in total. The inhabitants of Muhaga have never seen the contract. They never signed anything. They don't even know how much land in total has been handed over to Sun Biofuels: for the moment they have lost 1,705 hectares of the 5,767 they had at their disposal. A third of their land.[1] 'But they could take more in the future. Nobody has told us anything.'

The other ten villages have given up more or less the same percentage of their land; some 30 percent, some 35, some even 45. Some compensation has been paid, but the criteria used to establish the value of the land are not clear, nor is it clear why certain villages and certain private owners have received compensation, while others have not. 'We haven't seen a penny,' repeats Athumani. 'We're still waiting.'

Take the land and run

The property laws in Tanzania divide the land into three categories: 'reserved land', which is untouchable and belongs to the national parks or the natural and marine reserves; 'general' land, which the government can use as it sees fit; and 'village land', which, in accordance with custom, is the property of the local community that uses it. No foreigner can buy land, it can only be rented for a maximum period of ninety-nine years, and must belong to the 'general' category. According to the 1999 Village Land Act, it is forbidden to rent out land belonging to local communities. There is only one way to obtain this kind of land: by changing its designation from 'village' to 'general'.[2] This can only be done with the consent of the community affected and must also include the payment of compensation. Given that the vast majority of land in Tanzania falls into the 'village' category, the procedure followed by international investors in recent years has almost always been the same: to secure the *placet* of the communities, often with the direct support of the central government or some local representative, like the Kisarawe parliamentarian who managed to get the go-ahead from eleven villages by repeating eleven times the same three-card trick. The procedure, which in theory is complicated from a legal viewpoint, is in many cases effected by means of a short cut: the transfer takes place by oral consent, without formal documents. At the present time, many villages still don't know how much land they have actually ceded, or if they will ever get the money or the services they have been promised. The promises were made by word of mouth, without anything being formally written down. The only document the villagers in Muhaga have is a letter of intent on headed paper which states that the plan to guarantee 'clean water' for the eleven villages will soon be ready. 'But we still haven't seen anything,' cries a lady with a radiant face and an incredibly bright orange tunic, who is sitting beside the village chief. All my questions get the same answer from this volcanic, cheerful lady, who laughs as she repeats that 'no, no, no, nobody has come, nobody has taken on our case'. 'Have you been visited by any representatives from Sun Biofuels?' 'No.' 'Has anybody come from the district?' 'Nobody.' 'Have you seen the parliamentarian from Kisarawe since?' 'No.' 'Have you received any assurances about when the water pump will be built?' 'None.' The stream of *hapana* ('no') and *hakuna kitu* and *hakuna mtu* ('nothing' and 'nobody') is like machine-gun fire, so explicit that it speaks for itself, with no need for translation. The others around her nod their heads. Or rather, they nod 'no' every time the lady repeats *hapana*, which she enunciates so well, shouting it without anger, to make absolutely sure that the concept is clear. 'All they have said is that the water will arrive in the near future,' the village chief adds. But the villagers of Muhaga have come to understand that 'the near future' is a vague concept, especially when it concerns services that are supposed to benefit them.

Between the Tropic of Cancer and the Tropic of Capricorn

In recent years, Tanzania has become a destination of choice for foreign companies interested in developing agrofuels. The reasons for this are diverse: the European Commission's objective of replacing 10 percent of combustible fuel with renewable sources by 2020; the presence of a well-equipped and safe port in Dar es Salaam, from which the product can be exported; the political stability of the country as one of the few in the area that have not seen civil wars or post-electoral violence. Then there is the excellent climate and the low cost of labour. Added to all these are the same incentives that many African countries currently offer to attract investment: no duties on the importation of machinery, a five-year period of 'fiscal vacation' during which the company doesn't pay taxes on its returns, and other facilitations.

All things considered, Tanzania is a perfect example of one of those countries 'between the Tropic of Cancer and the Tropic of Capricorn' that the former Brazilian Minister for Agriculture, Roberto Rodrigues, has in mind: 'land-rich, full of sun and with a strong workforce, but poor in capital'. Rodrigues' vision – 'the capital will come from the north' – is already a reality in the Tanzanian countryside, especially in the coastal regions from which it is easier to export products. As well as Sun Biofuels, which started to operate here in 2009, there are also a number of other, largely European, companies that have rushed into this sector. They have all obtained village land. Some grow jatropha, others sugarcane for ethanol or palm oil. Since they are all still at the initial pre-export stage of their respective projects, it is not yet possible to put a figure on the profits that await them. In some cases, adequate compensation has been paid to all concerned, but in others, like the village of Muhaga, a dispute exists. The ways the companies have exploited the land varies: some have directly involved local cultivators in their enterprise; others, like the one in Kisarawe, have hired them as day labourers. Then there are those who have taken the land and run with their ill-begotten gains. One such is the Dutch company, Bioshape, which obtained a 34,000 hectare concession for ninety-nine years in the district of Kilwa, on the country's north coast. It razed the area, cut down all the trees and then, having sold all the wood for profit, abandoned the area. What was formerly an area of forestland is now bare and uncultivated. But it cannot now be cultivated, as it belongs to Bioshape, who are unlikely to do anything with it. In fact, according to Tanzanian law the land can no longer be returned to the village, because its transfer to the 'general' category is irreversible. At the very most, following a particularly complicated legal procedure, it may be given to the president, who can then pass it on to some other investor. To make matters worse, the villages were not given the entire amount of compensation Bioshape pledged, but only 40 percent of the figure. The other 60 percent was paid to the 'district council' in return for unspecified services.

This swindle by the Dutch firm is perfectly legal: the land was conceded in accordance with Tanzanian regulations. Since then the company has been declared formally bankrupt and has abandoned the project. In fact, according to work done by investigative journalists, the entire agrofuel operation was merely a ruse, as the investors concerned had simply planned all along to make easy money from the sale of the wood.[3]

This is also confirmed to me by Finnigan Wa Simbeye, a Tanzanian journalist who has followed closely the development of biofuels in his country. 'The government is corrupt, and only looks after itself', he tells me without providing any more details. A smiling forty year old, Finnigan has worked for the past ten years as an investigative journalist for *The Daily News*, as well as collaborating regularly with the specialised newsletter *Africa Confidential* and with *The Africa Report*, an English supplement of the Parisian weekly magazine *Jeune Afrique*. Having read his detailed articles on the internet, I broke one of the unwritten rules of behaviour for journalists: 'Never call a colleague and ask him for a favour if you don't know him personally.' But I wanted to ask Finnigan for more information on the stories he had told so well, especially that of Sun Biofuels at Kisarawe, which I was hoping to visit. He was friendly on the phone and suggested we meet at eight o'clock that evening at the Millennium Tower, a commercial centre on one of the main arteries of Dar es Salaam. I arrive for our appointment right on time. The commercial centre, a vaguely art deco building with three floors, is closed. The place is silent and deserted. I sit outside a little bar next door and order a Sprite. I'm immediately attacked by a swarm of moths, attracted by the only light source in the area. There are hundreds of them. They set upon me and the other two unfortunate clients at the bar, who are also probably waiting for someone. The insects get everywhere: they flap their wings off the notebook I'm scribbling on, jump around the table, bounce off my feet. At first I try to squash them, but soon I get used to their presence and don't pay them any heed. I close my notebook and take a drink, closing the bottle lid after every slug to keep the moths out. Finnigan arrives forty minutes late. He sits down without ordering anything, offers me a curt apology and lets me know that he doesn't have much time. He answers my questions on Kilwa and Kisarawe without adding anything that wasn't already in his articles. He says that the managers at Sun Biofuels are 'thugs who even threatened me', something he has already written.[4] When I ask him for some figures on Kisarawe, he says that unfortunately he has lost them. Less than twenty minutes later we are saying goodbye and expressing the clearly insincere desire to 'stay in touch'. I make a mental note that the rule about never calling a local journalist unless you've already met him, are offering a collaboration, or want to hire him as a fixer, is a hard and fast one which must be respected. I can't blame Finnigan for his lack of cooperation. I realise that I'd probably behave the same way if some foreign colleague turned up from nowhere pursuing a big story that just happened to be my speciality.

Journalists are extremely jealous of their discoveries and their sources – this is their private property and there's no way they'll share it unless there's something in it for them. So I walk off into the Dar es Salaam night, chiding myself for my naivety, and contemplating the virtues and vices of us journalists, a curious but selfish breed, distrustful by nature, but also capable of developing incredible passions and noble feelings of solidarity. Especially with those who can get us closer to that all-exclusive story.

From Berlin to Dar es Salaam

The next day, I go to visit Abdallah Mkindi. A tiny man with very short hair and a slight, almost imperceptible voice, Abdallah is one of the Directors of Envirocare, an NGO focusing on the environment and human rights that has been following the question of foreign investment in agriculture for years. I'd already met him at a conference on land grabbing in Berlin, at which he'd given a presentation on the many agrofuel development projects in Tanzania. The conference was organised by a number of organisations who are following this issue closely and, together with a Latin-American activist, Mkindi received a hero's welcome: he was a militant from the south who had come to tell the Europeans about what the neo-colonialist capitalists from their countries were doing down there. He was a real live witness of a phenomenon that most of the participants – the room was packed with over three hundred people – had only read about in newspaper articles. At the same conference Thomas Koch – a representative of a German investment fund who showed admirable bravery by throwing himself into this cauldron of hostility – faced a firing line of questioning over his activities and the immoral nature of the operations he was financing. The afternoon I spent in that crowded little room was both enjoyable and very educational. I had witnessed a conflict between two opposing and yet equally idealistic viewpoints: on the one hand Koch, representing the proponents of the 'green revolution' or large-scale investments in agriculture; on the other, the vast majority of those attending, militants from European organisations that consider every intervention in the south an act of daylight robbery. Koch was greeted with laughter and several whistles when he said that Germany had also received millions of dollars in foreign investment after the Second World War. Comparing investments in agriculture in Africa by European capital to the Marshall Plan was certainly an unfortunate blunder, but the man showed the same conviction and unbending faith that I had seen in the eyes of the investors I had met only a few days previously in Geneva. He also cited the inevitable World Bank 'principles for responsible development' as a sort of infallible *vedeme-cum* for avoiding the problems that all the other speakers had brought to light. As I listened to the speeches – as well as the two foreign guests, other journalists, university professors and researchers had also given presentations – I looked around at the reactions in the room. This conference was the exact opposite of the one I had been to in Geneva: Koch was the intruder in Berlin whereas in Geneva the intruders were members of organisations critical of irresponsible investments in agriculture, whose speeches had been strategically positioned after all the others. Berlin was the other side of Geneva. These two conferences confirmed the comments that an FAO official had made to me – 'off the record, please' – some time before. 'The problem is that in these discussions there is no middle ground, only two extremes: those who want investment at all cost, and those who consider any investment an act of neo-colonialism,' said the official, who also believed his organisation's position to be 'uncritical and leaning too far in the direction of the first extreme'. The more toned-down voices that did not belong to either of these two poles were rare, and therefore caught my attention. Mkindi could be considered one of these. His presentation had covered expropriation and the predatory projects undertaken by European firms in Tanzania, with photos and slides. But he'd also underlined how his country was in the middle of a deep crisis due to the collapse in value of its cash crops (in this case, cotton and coffee) on the world markets, leading to a fall in earnings for small farmers and in the amount of strong currency the government could obtain from the export of these products. He had explained, in other words, that agriculture in Tanzania is in crisis for structural reasons and not merely because of intervention by foreign companies. In a nation in which the agricultural sector accounts for 80 percent of the work force, 85 percent of exports and 25 percent of GDP, the question called for more than simple ideology. Mkindi hadn't offered solutions – this wasn't his role – but he had clearly laid out the problem, and shown that the situation was much more complex than was being suggested by the opposing sides, personified by the investors in Geneva (and Koch in Berlin) and by the representatives of civil society who had come together in the German capital on this cold and rainy November afternoon.

At the end of his speech, I introduced myself and told him I planned to visit his country two months later precisely to research the situation regarding the assignment of land to foreigners and projects related to agrofuels. 'Call me as soon as you arrive in Dar es Salaam,' he said enthusiastically. 'I'd be happy to give you a hand.' Needless to say, as soon as I land in the Tanzanian capital I do just that. In his barely audible voice he says that he remembers me well and asks me to come to his office that afternoon. 'We can meet at 4.30. I've got about half an hour,' he says, a little hurriedly, and in a very different tone to the one in which he had said goodbye in Berlin, when he handed me his card and added, 'See you in Dar.'

When the time comes, I make my way to the suburban area where the Envirocare office is located. After a seemingly endless ride on a *dala-dala* – the shabby but generally efficient little vans that provide public transport on the long and dusty streets of Dar es Salaam – a taxi takes me down to the bottom of a steep dirt road and a small wooden house surrounded by a neatly kept garden. The Envirocare headquarters is welcoming. Two rooms full of computers and a library in which some students are presumably doing some research. Abdallah introduces me to his colleagues, and we then start to talk about my project. His approach towards me seems contradictory: his manners are cold and a little stand-offish. He doesn't appear to listen too carefully to what I'm saying and gives off an air of being in a hurry, as if he can't wait for me to leave his office. When I tell him that I want to go to Kisarawe, however, he looks me right in the eye and says, 'Wait a minute.' He starts tapping away at his compu-ter, then pulls up the telephone number of one of the villagers from Muhaga. He calls him, explaining who I am and what I want to do. Then he hands the phone to me. The man on the line speaks a little English, and tells me that he won't be there but that he will tell the others I am coming. The whole business takes less than three minutes. I hang up and thank Abdallah for his help, the kind of help I had looked for from Finnigan, fool-ishly expecting that a sense of solidarity between colleagues would suffice. As I say goodbye and thank him once again, I realise that Mkindi isn't aloof after all. He's just pragmatic, and really doesn't have time for small talk. 'I'd very much like to come with you,' he says to my surprise as he drives me back to the *dala-dala*. 'But I've too much work on at the moment.'

'The vision is the mission'

The Ministry of Energy and Minerals is located in an impos-ing seven-floor building in the heart of Dar es Salaam, a stone's throw from the port. An enormous inscription in yellow covers the entire width of the facade: *Wizara ya Nishati na Madini – Ministry of Energy and Minerals*. A white sign lower down indicates 'the vision' and 'the mission' of the Ministry, which are, respectively: 'To be an efficient institution, to contribute in a significant way to socioeconomic development through sustainable development and use of energy and mineral resources,' and 'to enact and monitor policies, strategies and laws for the sustainability of energy and mineral resources in order to facilitate economic growth and development.' I'm here to meet Styden Rwebangila, the manager of the Ministry's Biofuels Unit. I managed to make this appointment with surprising ease. I called the switchboard and asked to be put through to the Biofuels Department. A man answered and I explained who I was and asked if I could speak to the manager. He wasn't in his office, but after thinking about it for a couple of seconds the man then gave me the manager's mobile phone number. That's how I got through to Rwebangila who, after his initial surprise, asked me to come to the Ministry in exactly one hour. 'You can come straight to me in room 512.'

I arrive at the building on time and go inside. Nobody asks me anything. I'm heading towards the lift when the usher beckons me over. He shows me the visitors' book, and simply asks me to write my name and time of arrival. No security check. No questions. No ID necessary. Just a name written in ink in a notebook. Between the man giving me his boss's mobile number and now this, I come to the conclusion that Tanzania is one laid-back country. I make my way up to Rwebangila's office and knock on the door. It's opened by a man of about thirty-five, dressed in a dark shirt that doesn't hide a little excess weight, trousers with no belt, and trainers. 'Thank you for seeing me at such short notice,' I say. 'Not at all,' he answers. 'We are always happy to show what we do here to the foreign press.'

The Biofuels Unit was created by the government in 2005 to supervise a sector that up to then simply hadn't existed. Rwebangila is second in command: the Director is busy on a mission in Malawi and this leaves Rwebangila temporarily in charge of the office. As a young engineer with a Masters from Imperial College London, he was called upon to deal with the biofuels issue, a subject about which, as he freely admits, he initially 'knew little or nothing'. 'Over the past six years, we have learnt so much, and have defined strategic areas of intervention. We started at square one and have already made quite a bit of progress.' A Biofuel Task Force was created by putting together managers from the Ministry of Energy, the Ministry for Agriculture, the Tanzania Investment Centre, and representatives from the private sector. The most significant thing it has done in the last six years is produce an eighteen-page booklet, *Guidelines for the Sustainable Development of Biofuels in Tanzania*, a copy of which the engineer immediately hands me. The gestation period of this booklet was long and arduous, the result of lengthy negotiations and multiple rewritings. 'We were pressurised on all sides: by investors, who wanted a reference framework in which they could operate free from criticism, and by the civil society organisations, who were demanding that we regulate the sector.' The guidelines themselves are very advanced: they stipulate that land concessions for biofuel production should be for a maximum period of twenty-five years, with a five-year trial period; they actively encourage *contract farming*, or the direct involvement of small farmers in the enterprise; they forbid the forced movement of populations; and they require investors to present a feasibility study in consultation with all relevant local and national authorities.

There's only one problem: these guidelines are not binding. They are not backed up by law. 'They are a useful means for advancing the debate,' says Rwebangila, clearly aware that his work has had a limited impact. Most of the agrofuel development project launched in Tanzania in recent years have explicitly violated these guidelines: they have caused the displacement of populations; they are based on ninety-nine year leases; they have seen hardly any local authority involvement and included no feasibility studies. I ask him if the guidelines can be applied to projects that are already underway. He answers that it is up to the government to decide or, at the very least, the judiciary. 'We are technicians, we provide a picture of the situation and propose a number of strategies for action,' the engineer stresses, having noted the look of perplexity on my face.

'How many biofuel production projects are presently active in Tanzania?' I ask him. Rwebangila furrows his brow in thought. 'I couldn't put an exact figure on that.' I ask him for information on the Kilwa project (the one abandoned by the Dutch firm after they'd sold off all the wood) and on Kisarawe, which I had visited the day before. 'We are aware that there are problems. But they are not directly within our jurisdiction. We have been charged with analysing the sector and have defined guidelines, also on the basis of our experience over the past few years.' In fact, the booklet contains a sentence that seems like a direct reference to the Bioshape theft: 'Land is given to the investor on condition that it is only used for his declared objective.'

It's not entirely clear what role the unit run by Rwebangila actually performs, or what strategy it has developed over its six-year history. During our conversation, the engineer comes up with all kinds of contradictions. He says that agrofuels could be Tanzania's new cash crop, but adds that investments in the sector can be dangerous, because they can undermine food sovereignty and lead to potentially devastating land grabbing. He says they encourage plantations that aren't too big and are located in less fertile regions, but then acknowledges that practically all the present projects are in prime locations and spread over very large tracts of land. He says that the government doesn't favour investment, but then speaks about a direct collaboration with Petrobras – the Brazilian petroleum company – intended to acquire knowledge of the sector. Basically, it's hard to nail down the engineer's personal position with regard to agrofuels. Maybe he doesn't have one. Or perhaps he's trying to represent the unit he manages, while fully conscious of its structural limits and obscure role. As he talks, he clutches the little green guideline book in his hand, almost as if it were his saving grace, proof that his unit exists and has actually done something. 'We are just a small piece in a large mosaic. We try to do our best,' he mutters defensively as we say goodbye.

I leave the building, plunging back into the torrid heat of Dar es Salaam, and think back to the meeting I'd had the day before in Muhaga. I think about the enormous gap between those peasants who have seen their land taken from them and the members of a government agency who don't even know how many projects of this kind are active in Tanzania. I take another look at the building's facade, and my eyes fall once again to the inscription: 'Vision: to contribute in a significant way to socioeconomic development through sustainable development.' I read it over and over again, and realise that it means nothing.

The business of carbon credits

'The Biofuels Unit at the Ministry of Energy is a big hoax. It was created to gratify the investors.' Yefred Myenzi is the Director of HakiArdhi, a highly rated research centre in Tanzania that deals with land law. I go to visit him on a particularly leaden morning, with a white sky trapping the city in a low pressure grip. Yefred is a strong man with enormous shoulders, the face of a fighter like Mike Tyson, but without the marks left on the former World Champion from his life both in and outside the ring. His face is stocky but clean, his voice bombastic, his handshake firm. He is impeccably dressed: a black shirt with a pair of silver cufflinks, a yellow tie, and a pair of moccasins. His office is simple but unmistakably that of a boss: a large solid wooden desk, a modern computer, a telephone on a second desk and another small table behind which he asks me to sit. Then there is the air conditioning, which here as elsewhere in Africa predominantly serves as a symbol of power. The Director keeps it on fairly high, which allows him to remain all dressed up although it's absolutely boiling outside. He apologises for keeping me waiting. 'I just came back from abroad yesterday and have a backlog of work.' Yefred was at the World Social Forum in Dakar, Senegal, the annual meeting of the world's so-called civil society.

Launched in 2000 in Porto Alegre, Brazil, over the years it has become a little repetitive, and has lost much of its initial impetus. I have only been to one of these events, in Bamako, Mali's capital, in 2006; even then I got the impression that the formula had grown tired and was marked by assemblies in which the participants indulged themselves in insulting the reigning neoliberalism, but were incapable of more reflective analyses or of making concrete proposals. It seemed to me to be more celebratory than grounded in reality; there were many Europeans who were setting foot in Africa for the very first time, quite a few characters seeking to pass themselves off as leaders, several mavericks, and very few young people. All of which reinforced my congenital suspicion of meetings whose participants are largely in agreement with each other and all too convinced of the righteousness of their ideas.

To break the ice, I ask Yefred how the meeting in Dakar went. He answers that it's always an occasion to meet people and to network. But then he adds, lowering his gaze a little, that 'these events are fairly pointless, they are decidedly self-referential'. This comment creates a flash of empathy between us. I briefly tell him about my experience in Bamako, and he says that he was there too, and it was just like the one in Nairobi held the year after. The same was true this year, he tells me, in fact more so given that the Forum was being held while a popular revolution was overthrowing the Egyptian President, Hosni Mubarak: 'I had the impression of being in some kind of ivory tower, light years from real events and from the masses.'

'But let's get down to business. I'm sure you haven't come here to talk about the Social Forum,' he adds, smiling. His position on biofuels is clear and categorical: 'The government is playing dirty. It is tricking the small farmers, and giving away their land for a crust of bread and a few sweeteners.' Yefred says that land grabbing is a reality in Tanzania and that it is totally untrue that the government isn't actively seeking to attract investment. He tells me that by chance his wife ended up accompanying a vice-minister to a conference in South Africa, where the minister promoted investment in agriculture by announcing that 'in Tanzania the land is fertile and the cost of labour is extremely low'. I tell him that these are the exact same words I've heard in Riyadh from representatives from other African countries, and inform him of the downward-spiralling auction I had witnessed there. Then, aware that his institute has drawn up a very precise map of investments, I ask him about the present state of affairs in Tanzania.

He describes the various projects that are already underway and those that are presently being negotiated. 'Up to now, the Tanzania Investment Centre has conceded 640,000 hectares to foreign firms. There are three types of foreign investments in agriculture. The most important of these concern agrofuels. Then come investments related to food production for exportation, in which the Arab States and the Koreans are primarily involved. Finally, we have investments related to carbon credit.' This last topic is a less well-known aspect of land grabbing. According to the Clean Development Mechanism (CDM) set out as part of the Kyoto Protocol, a company from a developed country that exceeds its carbon dioxide quota can buy 'carbon credits' by sponsoring emission-reducing projects in developing countries. In other words, it can compensate for its over-polluting by limiting the presence of greenhouse gases in another part of the world. The intentions behind the setting up of this mechanism were good: the northern countries would finance sustainable development in the south because it would cost them less to support these projects than to reduce their own emissions up north. But the system was distorted: given that the signatories to the Kyoto Protocol were bound by specific targets to be met by 2012, carbon credits themselves have become a commodity, a merchandise subject to the mechanisms of financial speculation. As such, they are traded on various stock exchanges, complete with futures and options with annual expiries. The financialisation of the sector – and the prospects opened up by the targets laid down by Kyoto[5] – have enticed certain private companies to enter into an apparently very promising business venture: acquiring carbon credits in the south and then reselling them on the market. A number of firms have obtained land upon which they've planted trees, with the express purpose of acquiring 'reduction certificates'. Others are trying to kill the proverbial two birds with one stone by developing agrofuel cultivations that can be certified as emission-reducing projects by the CDM. In this way, they get to sell at a profit both the biofuel and the carbon credits.[6]

This financialisation of the system and the insertion of carbon credits into a pure market mechanism would not necessarily have been damaging, had it not brought about a deregulation of the sector, and the continuation of various projects without due consideration for local realities. A number of 'reforestation' projects have been undertaken merely to obtain credits, with excessive haste and little respect for the conditions of the local environment. For example, they may be undertaken in areas which were not previously forested, but were used for growing agricultural produce or for pasture. This was the case with the Mufindi region, in Southern Tanzania, where the Norwegian company Green Resources planted Eucalyptus trees on 2,600 hectares of village land ceded ad hoc by local communities. A case that Yefred knows well, as he is from the area. 'They leased the land. They planted many trees. The villagers are all happy: they received money for their land. But what they don't realise is that they have lost their primary resource. That the money will run out and they will find themselves watching the trees grow without being able to grow their crops.'[7] He stops for a minute, drums his fingers on the table, and then asks me rhetorically, 'In all of this, where is the benefit for the local communities?'

'Perhaps they can reinvest the money they've received as compensation?' I suggest. The Director smiles. Then his brow darkens and he takes on a more serious air. 'Of course, they could do that, but often they don't have the means and the culture to invest it in long-term projects or really think about their future.' Yefred offers the example of a village that, not really knowing what to do with its compensation money, bought a used truck with which to start a transport business. Six months later the truck broke down, and the business shut down. 'Now the village has an unusable truck at the side of the road, and its land is gone.'

The man has a broad understanding of the problem. He knows the situation in Tanzania well and is fully able to place it within a wider perspective. 'The question is a complex one,' he tells me, 'because it represents a global movement.

Nowadays, land has become a commodity. There are groups of speculators who consider the acquisition of a number of hectares in order to draw a profit from their use a way of making money without excessive risk. Perhaps there's a guy in Washington who decides that a particular plot in Tanzania is a better, and safer, investment than buying shares in a company that develops new technologies. And so he puts his money into this enterprise. He arrives. He promises the moon and the stars. Then, as soon as he makes a profit, he leaves. That's all there is to it. The peasants who lose their land, or are tricked, are just collateral damage in a movement that is infinitely bigger than them.' Yefred is not blaming the investors 'who are doing their job'. He is furious, however, with the politicians responsible. 'The government is myopic. It actively authorises and facilitates investments that are potentially devastating: either because it is corrupt, or because it sincerely thinks that attracting foreign investment can prove useful for the country's development. Either way, it is an active accomplice in land grabbing.' Yefred is by now beside himself with anger: it's clear that the subject is one he feels very strongly about. His institute has produced many studies on land acquisitions and on the risks embedded in the unregulated development of biofuels. So I ask him what he thinks of the guidelines on biofuels.

'The government has made an effort to regulate the sector,' I say to draw a reaction. Again he breaks out in a smile. Then he pulls out of a drawer the same little green book that Rwebangila had shown me. 'Have you read it?' he asks. I nod my head. 'Well? What's in here? Just words. The reality is different: people are being hunted from their land, compensation is not being paid, rental contracts are not for twenty-five years but for a century, there is no real control over the actions of these foreign companies. In other words, this booklet is wastepaper.'

'So why have they produced it?' 'What do you think these guidelines are for?' he asks. Then he continues, without waiting for an answer, caught up in his reasoning. 'These guidelines only serve the investors, in order to put their conscience at ease. They can say: we have followed the guidelines, even if it isn't true. As for the government, well they can say to their critics: it's not true that we are giving away the land for nothing, we have even written these guidelines!'

'Future generations will burn your tombs'

Perhaps the guidelines were drawn up just to silence the critics of foreign investment in agrofuels. But one thing is certain: criticism, at least in Tanzania, is not exactly virulent. Apart from the organisations I visited, a handful of journalists and those directly affected by the phenomenon, no one else I talked to who knew about the land grabbing that was happening in the country seemed particularly scandalised by it. The subject doesn't get much coverage in the press. It's seen as a distant, technical problem, related to unpaid compensation to rural communities. In contrast with Ethiopia, where the various opponents of the government abroad have created a change in opinion, in these parts it is not really discussed.

This may seem like a paradox: Tanzania is an open country, with a relative freedom of the press and freedom of expression. Unlike Ethiopia, here people can say whatever they want, without risking arrest or losing their jobs. But the paradox is not real. If a closed political system obstructs the spread of information, this actually increases discussion. In Ethiopia I could never have visited a village like Muhaga and spoken freely with everybody, because every village has a government party representative who would have immediately informed the authorities or told the villagers to keep their mouths shut. Outside of Ethiopia, however, there were international campaigns against the land grabbing going on there. In an almost totalitarian regime like that in Ethiopia, in which every dissenting voice is nipped at the bud, opposition to land grabbing is primarily seen as opposition to the government. Land grabbing, therefore, is something that everybody knows about, even if no one in the country will dare talk about it openly. In the Tanzanian countryside I was able to talk with whoever I wanted, and to gather whatever information I needed. But then I realised that, apart from the experts, nobody seemed all that hot under the collar or was rushing to denounce the government for ceding large tracts of land for next to nothing.

I saw no organised movements, social pressure or national solidarity. The small farmers seem resigned to their fate, having come up against a force much stronger than themselves. The villagers at Muhaga surprised me when I asked them: 'What do you intend to do?' 'Nothing, what can we do?' they answered. The idea of organising protests in the capital, contacting lawyers, or fighting for their rights hadn't seemed to cross their minds. They hadn't even formed a network with the other ten villages that had been treated the same way. At first, I was dumbfounded by this total lack of initiative. But then I realised that I was projecting my urban mentality upon people who had neither running water nor electricity. The universe, for the Muhaga villagers, is their village. The central government is a faraway entity that only ever intervenes to give them orders. They know that they have been tricked by the Kisarawe parliament, but they see this injustice as a travesty that cannot be fixed, like a harvest destroyed by a hailstorm or some unknown parasite. This is perhaps the clearest illustration of the enormous gap that exists between two worlds that are so distant and yet now so geographically near: the peasant, unaware that his land has now become a commodity, and the investor sitting in his office in Washington DC, thinking that it might be better to invest in jatropha than in dot.com enterprises.

The gap between these two worlds lies at the very heart of the problem, and is the common thread that links the conversations I have had, the people I have met, and the situations I have seen across the four corners of the world. The great land rush feeds primarily on differences in knowledge and means; it is gauged and articulated in the distance that separates rural populations who have lived undisturbed for years in their fields, and certain characters who appear out of nowhere promising them development and a route to well-being that inevitably seduces them. In the various forms and shades it has taken, depending on the context or the latitude, land grabbing is essentially an enormous deception that deprives small farmers of their land and livelihoods, either through procedures imposed by the authorities, like in Ethiopia, or through conjurors' tricks like in Tanzania. The view held by the participants at the Berlin conference was one I basically shared: the rural areas in the south are playing host to a modern form of neo-colonialism. The former colonies are now being conquered by old and new powers. As in colonial times, these powers are hunting overseas for the resources they need, for food to feed their own people, and for fuel to keep their cars on the road. After all, isn't the initiative set up by Saudi Arabia's King Abdullah – with its exploration missions abroad, its agents on the ground, and its aggressive land-acquisition policy – comparable to the old East India Company? Aren't the investors who come to plant jatropha in Tanzania essentially new Conquistadores, ensnaring the locals with promises of a new school or hospital?

But the core issue, the fulcrum of the question, lies elsewhere. Yefred Myenzi was right: the primary culprits in this indiscriminate selling-off of land are the national governments, who barter their nations' resources for a fistful of strong currency – or, in the worst cases, for a bank transfer in dollars into an overseas bank account. The colonial era is over. Former colonies are now independent. But their governments are simply not looking after the interests of their citizens.

Making my way back from HakiArdhi's office, the sky blackens as a storm looms. As I get off the *dala-dala*, light rain starts to fall on the capital. A couple of minutes later, it has become a torrential downpour. My hotel, just fifty metres away, is unreachable: access is blocked by a river of water and mud. I sit down at a little bar and wait for it to end. I look at the rain falling and the devastating effect it has on this urban landscape. It strikes me that someone who lives here in Dar es Salaam has other priorities besides expressing solidarity with rural peasants who are being dispossessed of their land. Here, it is every man for himself. This is what deceives the government into thinking it can pass on the task of stimulating agricultural development to European investors, despite not having been able to do so itself in fifty years of independence.

Still watching the river that's stopping me from returning to the hotel, I think back to the presentation that Abdallah Mkindi gave in Berlin. At the end of his speech, he showed a couple of disturbing slides: the first was of a green plain covered with jatropha plants, which created a sense of immense desolation. The second had the same image in the background, but this time there was an inscription: 'Future generations will burn your tombs for leaving them without land.' My thoughts turn to the Muhaga peasants. Their population will grow, but they have two-thirds of the land they had two years ago. There's no guarantee that they won't have even less one year from now. A number of their children will find it impossible to survive where they were born. Perhaps they will leave for the cities, to swell even further the numbers of those who scrape a living as street traders. Or perhaps they will end up as day workers for the same companies that now control the land that once was theirs. I don't know if they will burn their ancestors' graves. But they will surely remember the year in which the village assembly gave their land away in return for nothing.

Appendix I: Updates on the Web

Given that land grabbing is a relatively new subject, it may be useful to list a few website addresses for keeping track of the phenomenon. Many of the sites listed here already appear in the text or in the footnotes of the book.

farmlandgrab.org: a thorough press review site that follows all reports related to land grabbing, and is run by the NGO Grain.

grain.org: the website of the NGO that for the past three years has brought attention to the land-grabbing phenomenon.

landcoalition.org: the website of the International Land Coalition, a consortium of international organisations, based in Rome, which works for fair access to land.

fao.org: the website for the United Nations Agency for Food and Agriculture.

oaklandinstitute.org: a research centre, based in California, which has carried out many studies on food sovereignty and on agricultural investments.

viacampesina.org: the website for an organisation which is a consortium of small farmer associations from all over the world.

ifpri.org: the website for the International Food Policy Research Institute, a Washington-based research centre whose mission is 'to find sustainable solutions that will end hunger and poverty'.

earth-policy.org: the website of the Earth Policy Institute, a Washington research centre founded and run by Lester Brown.

soyatech.com: a group that organises networking conferences for agricultural investors in the United States and Europe.

iied.org: the website for the International Institute for Environment and Development, a research centre based in London which has conducted many studies on land grabbing.

Notes

Chapter 1. Ethiopia: An Eldorado for Investors

1 Meles Zenawi died suddenly on 21 August 2012, leaving great uncertainty over the political future of Ethiopia in his wake.

2 See saudieastafricanforum.org

3 *Addis Fortune*, 12 October 2009.

4 For a detailed examination of the various land regimes in Ethiopia, from Haile Selassie's imperial era to the DERG period and the stipulation in the 1995 Constitution, see Wibke Crewett, Ayalneh Bogale and Benedikt Korf, 'Land Tenure in Ethiopia: Continuity and Change, Shifting Rulers, and the Quest for State Control', CAPRI Working Paper, September 2008, available at capri.cgiar.org.

5 Human Rights Watch, 'One Hundred Ways of Putting Pressure. Violations of Freedom of Expression and Association in Ethiopia', 24 March 2010, available at hrw.org.

6 On the political use the Ethiopian government makes of humanitarian aid, see Helen Epstein's essay, 'Cruel Ethiopia', *New York Review of Books*, 14 April 2010.

7 Birtukan Mideksa was freed in October 2010 after making a formal request for forgiveness.

8 For an 'insider's' criticism of this approach and an in-depth examination of the distortions caused by the influx of aid over the past thirty years throughout sub-Saharan Africa, see Dambisa Moyo, *Dead Aid: Why Aid is Not Working and How There is Another Way for Africa*, London: Allen Lane 2009.

9 See addisnegeronline.com.

10 As heard by the author, Addis Ababa, May 2010.

11 Even before overthrowing Mengistu, the Tigrinya rebels from the Tigrinyan People's Liberation Front (TPLF) formed the EPRDF, a sort of coalition which included three other 'ethnic' parties, the Amhara National Democratic Movement (ANDM), the Oromo People's Democratic Organisation (OPDO), and the Southern Ethiopia People's Democratic Movement (SEPDM). These parties represent the elite who, over the years, accepted Tigrinyan dominance at national level in return for power over their respective areas and a limited say with regard to the Federation's policies. For 'ethnic federalism' and its implications, see the report by the International Crisis Group, 'Ethiopia: Ethnic Federalism and its Discontents', 4 September 2009, available at crisisgroup.org, and for a historical and comparative perspective, David Turton (ed.), *Ethnic Federalism: The Ethiopian Experience in Comparative Perspective*, London: James Currey 2006.

12 'Five more years', *The Economist*, 20 May 2010.

13 'World Leaders Are Taking Notice of Land in Debre Zeit', *Capital*, 28 December 2009.

14 The COMESA is a free trade area which includes twenty African countries, from Libya to Zimbabwe. Of these, only fourteen have fully signed up, eliminating duties on imports and exports. Ethiopia is not among them, but negotiations are ongoing (see comesa.int).

15 Jason McLure, 'Ethiopian Farms Lure Investor Funds as Workers Live in Poverty', *Bloomberg News*, 31 December 2009, available at farmlandgrab.org.

16 Ministry of Mines and Energy, 'The Biofuel Development and Utilization Strategy of Ethiopia', available at phe-ethiopia.org.

17 sunbiofuels.com. For this company's activities in Tanzania, see below, Chapter 6, note 1.

18 Much of the information on the development of biofuels in Ethiopia was taken from the report by the environmental NGO Melca, 'Rapid Assessment of Biofuels Development Status in

Ethiopia and Proceedings of the National Workshop on Environmental Impact Assessment and Biofuels', September 2008, available at melca-ethiopia.org, and from a conversation with the Director of the organisation, Million Belay, Addis Ababa, May 2010.

19 For a detailed account of the whole Gilgel Gibe II story, from the granting of the contract to the collapse of the tunnel, see Stefano Liberti and Emilio Manfredi, 'La diga di cartapesta', 'The Papier Mâché Dam', *Il Manifesto*, 17 March 2010.

20 An international campaign is fighting against the financing of the Gilgel Gibe III Dam, coordinated by the NGO International Rivers and by Campagna per la Riforma della Banca Mondiale (Campaign for the Reform of the World Bank). For the impact of the dam on the local communities, see the detailed reports by CRBM (crbm.org) and the website stopgibe3.org.

21 Terry Hathaway, 'Silencing Dam Critics in Ethiopia', *Ethiopian Review*, 27 April 2010, available at ethiopianreview.com.

22 The study is available online at assets.survivalinternational.org.

Chapter 2. Saudi Arabia: Sheikhs on a Land Conquest

1 For precise data on Saudi grain production and subsidies, see the PowerPoint presentation used during a speech by the Vice-Minister for Agriculture at a conference on food security in Salzburg on 10 and 11 May 2009: 'Wheat Production in Saudi Arabia (A Three Decade Story)', available at agritrade.org.

2 This was the price that the USSR paid in 1979 for a tonne of grain imported from the United States. Cited in Padma Desai, 'Estimate of Soviet Grain Imports in 1980–85: Alternative Approaches', a study by the International Food Policy Research Institute, February 1981.

3 For details on KAISAIA, including Saudi Arabian food import requirements, see the presentation by Engineer Taha A. Alshareef at the 2009 Food Security Conference in Salzburg, available at agritrade.org.

4 Souhail Karam, 'Saudi-Based Partners Launch Africa Rice Farming Plan', Reuters, 3 August 2009, available at farmland-grab.org.

5 Andrew England, 'Riyadh Paves Way for Foreign Ventures', *Financial Times*, 24 May 2009.

6 See 'China's Africa Land Grab Myths Part II: The (Non-Existent) $5 Billion Fund', available at the blog chinaafricarealstory.com, by Deborah Brautigam, author of *The Dragon's Gift: The Real Story of China in Africa*, Oxford: Oxford University Press 2010.

7 For China's intervention policy in Africa, analysed from a very detailed historical perspective, see Deborah Brautigam's book, cited above.

8 Quoted by Stephen Marks in 'China and the Great Global Land Grab', *Pambazuka News*, 11 December 2008, available at pambazuka.org.

9 Many different figures have been given for this agreement. According to several accounts that appeared in the Congolese Press since 2007, ZTE, the Chinese company specialising in tele-communications, obtained 3 million hectares to grow palm trees for the industrial production of biofuels. This was only partially confirmed when the Council of Ministers in Kinshasa approved the lease of 100,000 hectares to ZTE. The project, which would represent the largest investment in agriculture by a Chinese company in Africa, still hasn't begun more than three years after the signing of the 'protocol of understanding' between the Congolese government and ZTE. For a detailed account of the agreement, see Deborah Brautigam's blog article, 'China and the African Land Grab: The DRC Oil Palm Deal', 15 March 2010, available at chinaafricarealstory.com.

10 Jamil Anderlini, 'China Eyes Overseas Land in Food Push', *Financial Times*, 8 May 2008.

11 Lorenzo Cotula, Sonja Vermeulen, Rebecca Leonard and James Keeley, 'Land Grab or Development Opportunity? Agriculture Investment and International Land Deals in Africa', International

Institute for Environment and Development (IFAD), Food and Agriculture Organisation (FAO) and International Fund for Agricultural Development (IFAD), London-Rome 2009.

12 Anti-Beijing sentiment explodes sporadically in countries where the Chinese presence is more entrenched. Particularly in Zambia, where the opposition candidate for the 2006 election, Michael Sata, based his entire campaign on his opposition to the Chinese presence in the northern copper belt. In the next election campaign, in 2011, Sata took a more moderate line and upon being elected President set about developing bilateral relations with China.

13 Press conference in Wade, Lisbon, 9 December 2007, observed in person by the author.

14 The Binladin Group showed an interest in developing a vast 500,000 hectare rice-growing plantation in Indonesia, but the project didn't come to pass. See Mita Valina Liem, 'Binladin Freezes Plans to Invest in Local Rice', *The Jakarta Globe*, 3 March 2009.

15 The nations in the Gulf Cooperation Council, a free trade area on the Arabian Peninsula, are Saudi Arabia, the United Arab Emirates, Qatar, Bahrain, Kuwait and Oman.

16 According to a cable published by the WikiLeaks site, the agreement broke down because the Chinese were interested in building the port as part of a more general infrastructure project that also involved Ethiopia and South Sudan. Samwel Kumba, 'How China Pushed Qatar out of Sh400bn Lamu Port Deal', *The Daily Nation*, 10 December 2010, available at farmlandgrab.org.

17 Contract farming involves a contract between a large investor and groups of small farmers. The former promises to buy, at a prearranged price, a percentage of the harvest. The latter promise to produce the quantity of the crop that was agreed upon in the contract.

18 An acre is approximately 0.4 of a hectare.

Chapter 3. Geneva: The Financiers of Arable Land

1 The Committee on Food Security (CFS) is a United Nations advisory body created in the 1970s to put in place policies aimed at guaranteeing world food security. It meets yearly at the FAO headquarters in Rome. See fao.org/cfs.

2 FAO, 'How to Feed the World in 2050', Rome, 2009, available at fao.org.

3 See farmlandgrab.org. The site reviews the papers in great detail and in several languages, and analyses all land acquisition contracts or projects that are reported.

4 'Daewoo to Cultivate Madagascar Land for Free', *Financial Times*, 19 November 2008.

5 The President who succeeded Ravalomanana, Andry Rajoelina, annulled the contract, but didn't go as far as to declare a moratorium on land leasing. In fact, the constitution approved by referendum in November 2010 makes provision for the possibility of renting and selling land to foreigners 'in accordance with the modalities laid down by the law'. Many land transfer projects are presently suspended due to political instability, which is deterring international investors. See the Collectif pour la Déffense des Terres Malgaches, at terresmalgaches.info.

6 '50 People Who Could Save the Planet', *Guardian*, 5 January 2008.

7 On the implications extensive palm oil plantations have for the environment and biodiversity in Indonesia and Malaysia, see Ian MacKinnon, 'Palm Oil: the Biofuel of the Future Driving an Ecological Disaster Now', *Guardian*, 4 April 2007.

8 '50 People Who Could Save the Planet', *Guardian*, 5 January 2008.

9 On the role played by the International Finance Corporation in promoting land acquisition, especially in Africa, read the report by the Oakland Institute, '(Mis)Investment in Agriculture: The Role of the International Finance

Corporation in Global Land Grabs', April 2010, available at oaklandinstitute.org,

10 For analysis on the World Bank's role in these projects and the way it works generally, see the reports by the Italian NGO, Campagna per la Riforma della Banca Mondiale (crbm.org) and a book written by two members of this NGO, Luca Manes and Antonio Tricarico, *La banca dei Ricchi. Perché la World Bank non ha sconfitto la povertà*, Rome: Terre di Mezzo 2008.

11 World Bank, 'Rising Global Interest in Farmland: Can it Yield Sustainable and Equitable Benefits?', Washington DC, September 2010, available at www.donorplatform.org. For a methodological critique of the World Bank report see 'World Bank Report on Land Grabbing: Beyond the Smoke and Mirrors', Grain, September 2010, available at grain.org.

12 Following the publication of the report, the *Financial Times* claimed that 'The World Bank supports investment in agriculture' (Javier Bias, 'World Bank Backs Investments in Global Farmland', *Financial Times*, 7 December 2010). Bloomberg, for its part, only went as far as saying that the agreements put at risk local control of access to land: Sandrine Rastello, 'Large Land Deals Threaten Farmers', Bloomberg, 8 September 2010, available at bloomberg.com.

13 World Bank, 'Rising Global Interest in Farmland: Can it Yield Sustainable and Equitable Benefits?', pp. 102–3.

14 For a detailed list of the RAI principles see responsibleagroinvestment.org.

15 For an articulate critique of the RAI principles by the most active peasant organisations in the South see viacampesina.org.

16 See srfood.org/images/stories/pdf/otherdocuments/20090611_large-scale-land-acquisitions-en.pdf.

17 See ngpgap.com.

18 Brian O'Keefe, 'Betting the Farm', *Fortune Magazine*, 8 June 2009.

19 Cargill invests in land acquisitions through its subsidiary, Black

River Asset Management. Louis Dreyfuss participates in land acquisitions in South America through the specialised fund, Calyx Agro. See the list of the companies implicated in the affair that Grain published at grain.org.

20 For a detailed analytical list of the financial instruments, companies and funds involved in land acquisition, see the report by the consultation firm Merian Research and CRBM, 'The Vultures of Land Grabbing. The Involvement of European Financial Companies in Large-Scale Land Acquisition Abroad', available at rinoceros.org.

21 'IFC Provides $75 mn Support for Altima Agri Fund', *Commodity Online*, 16 February 2009, available at commodityonline.com.

22 For a list of the agricultural projects that the World Bank is directly involved in, whether through the IFC or through MIGA, see 'World Bank Report on Land Grabbing: Beyond the Smoke and Mirrors', available at grain.org.

23 See emergentasset.com. The company is present in South Africa, Zambia, Zimbabwe, Swaziland and Mozambique, and aims to extend into Angola, Namibia and Tanzania. Susan Payne recently sold her shares in Emergent Asset Management and founded EmVest, a similar investment fund (see emvest.com).

Chapter 4. Chicago: The Hunger Market

1 For the importance of the railway in Chicago's development, see Marco D'Eramo, *The Pig and the Skyscraper: Chicago, A History of our Future*, London: Verso 2003.

2 The bushel is the measurement used in the United States for primary food produce. Given that it's a volumetric unit – equal to the capacity of a cylinder 18.5 inches (46.99 cm) in diameter and 8 inches (20.32 cm) in height – the corresponding quantity varies depending on the product. Convention holds that a bushel equals 27.216 kg of grain, 21.772 kg of barley, 25.301 kg of rye, 14.515 kg of oats.

3 His story inspired Frank Norris's novel *The Pit* (New York:

Doubleday, Page & Co 1903), which explains perfectly the way the stock market works, as well as offering a brilliant portrayal of the environment in which the big speculators moved at the beginning of the last century.

4 See www.cmegroup.com.

5 Most of these – 83 percent of 10.8 million contracts in July 2010 – are negotiated on the electronic platform (see www.cmegroup.com).

6 Beat Balzli and Frank Hornig, 'The Role of Speculators in the Global Food Crisis', *Der Spiegel*, 23 April 2008.

7 See patrickarbor.com.

8 At the end of 2011, Congress did not renew the 45 cent per gallon federal subsidies on ethanol production but still maintained the targets for increased ethanol production set out in the Renewable Fuel Standard Act.

9 On the presumed sinister reasons for this change of policy, read the interesting article by F. William Engdahl, 'The Hidden Agenda Behind Bush's Biofuel Plan', *Counterpunch*, 13 August 2007, available at counterpunch.org.

10 An American gallon is equal to 3.79 litres.

11 The figures are supplied by the Renewable Fuels Association, ethanolrfa.org.

12 Rick Perry, 'Texas is Fed Up with Corn Ethanol', *Wall Street Journal*, 12 August 2008, available at online.wsj.com.

13 The Low Carbon Fuel Standard law adopted in April 2009 stipulates that from 2011 fuel used in California must have a decreasing effect on carbon dioxide emissions. The calculation takes into consideration the entire production line of the fuel, including the potential emission of greenhouse gases from deforestation or from the conversion of land to biofuel cultivation. See the related article by Timothy Gardner, 'California Rule Could End Ethanol's Honeymoon', Reuters, 24 April 2009, available at reuters.com.

14 Alec MacGillis, 'Obama's Evolving Ethanol Rhetoric', *Washington Post*, 23 June 2008.

15 During the 2012 Presidential election campaign, the Republican candidate Mitt Romney declared himself to be in favour of the objectives set out in the Renewable Fuel Standard Act, thus forming a bipartisan line with his Democratic rival. This position did not take into consideration appeals by Governors of many southern states – as well as that of the FAO Secretary General – for a revision of the Standards.

16 Donald Mitchell, 'A Note on Rising Food Prices', World Bank, Policy Research Working Paper no.4682, July 2008, available at wds.worldbank.org. The World Bank later revised its position on this, claiming that 'the effects of biofuels on food prices have not been as significant as originally estimated'. See John Baffes and Tassos Haniotis, 'Placing the 2006/08 Commodity Price Boom into Perspective', World Bank, Policy Research Working Paper no. 5371, July 2010, available at elibrary.worldbank.org.

17 See in particular the study by the Massachusetts Institute of Technology which clearly shows the environmental cost of a biofuels program: Jerry M. Melillo, Angelo C. Gurgel, David W. Kicklighter, John M. Reilly, Timothy W. Cronin, Benjamin S. Felzer, Sergey Paltzev, C. Adam Schlosser, Andrei P. Sokolov and X. Wang, 'Unintended Environmental Consequences of a Global Biofuels Program', Report no. 168, January 2009, available at globalchange.mit.edu.

18 For an overview of various studies that highlight the benefits and defects of biofuels, see Kurt Kleiner, 'The Backlash Against Biofuels', *Nature*, 12 December 2007.

19 Lester R. Brown, *Plan B 3.0. Mobilizing to Save Civilisation*, New York: W. W. Norton & Company Inc. 2008.

20 Available at www.fao.org.

Chapter 5. Brazil: The Reign of Agribusiness

1 Conselho Indigenista Missionário (CIMI), 'Violência contra os povos indígenas no Brasil', 2008, available at cimi.org.br.

2 There were thirty-four Guarani murdered in 2008 alone, a rate

of 159.9 cases per 100,000 inhabitants in the 20–29 age bracket, compared with the national average of 6.1. See the report by Survival International, 'Violations of the Rights of the Guarani of Mato Grosso do Sul State, Brazil', March 2010, available at assets.survival-international.org.

3 With regard to the concentration of influence in the food industry and the ways in which agribusiness multinationals deploy their power, see Bill Vorley, 'Food Inc. Corporate Concentration from Farm to Consumer', IIED report, London 2003, available at ukfg.org.uk.

4 Quoted in Brewster Keen, *Invisible Giant: Cargill and its Transnational Strategies*, London: Pluto Press 2002. Essential reading for understanding both the mechanisms and degree of involvement of the world's leading agribusiness company.

5 The Lula government authorised this by Presidential decree: in 2002–3 it legalised the GMO harvests that had already been extensively planted. Today, two thirds of the soya grown in Brazil is GMO.

6 The European ban is nonetheless bypassed: genetically modified soya is given as feed to animals, and therefore indirectly ingested by European consumers who eat meat.

7 Regarding land concentration with respect to soya cultivation, see the report by the NGO Reporter Brazil, 'O Brasil dos agrocombustíveis. Soia, mamona', 2008, part of a lengthy field study by this association of independent journalists on the impact of agrofuels on the environment and on society (available at reporterbrasil.org.br).

8 Quoted in Maria Luisa Mendonça, 'Impacts of Expansion of Sugarcane Monocropping for Ethanol Production', from the report 'Impactos de produção de cana no Cerrado e Amazônia', 2008, published with the support of the Comissão Pastoral da Terra e la Rede Social de Justiça e Direitos Humanos, available at grassrootsonline.org.

9 For a detailed history of the Proálcool programme and the implications of ethanol production in Brazil, see John Wilkinson and

Selena Herrera, 'Biofuels in Brazil: Debates and Impacts', *Journal of Peasant Studies*, vol. 37, no. 4, October 2010.

10 According to the 'EU Energy Package', approved in December 2008 and acknowledged in the Renewable Energy Directive, by 2020 20 percent of energy used in the European Union must come from renewable sources (biomasses, bioliquids and biogases) and 10 percent of the fuel used in tyre transport must come from renewable energy. For a close examination of these European targets, the discussions that preceded their approval, and of a number of policies subsequently set in place, see Jennifer Franco, Les Levidow, David Fig, Lucia Goldfarb, Mireille Hönicke and Maria Luisa Mendonça, 'Assumptions in the European Union Biofuels Policy: Frictions with Experiences in Germany, Brazil and Mozambique', *Journal of Peasant Studies*, vol. 37, no. 4, October 2010.

11 The Central America Free Trade Agreement (CAFTA) – renamed DRCAFTA after the Dominican Republic joined it – is a free trade agreement between the United States and the Central American states of Guatemala, Honduras, Costa Rica, Nicaragua and El Salvador.

Chapter 6. Tanzania: The Frontier for Biofuels

1 Sun Biofuels went bankrupt in September 2011. The contract to Kisarawe was regained by another company, 30 Degrees East, which has not yet resumed operations. The workers who had been employed on the farms are still without work and without the possibility of cultivating the land that belonged to him.

2 For a detailed analysis of the land regime in Tanzania with regard to new investments, especially in the agrofuels sector, see Emmanuel Sule and Fred Nelson, 'Biofuel, Land Access and Rural Livelihoods in Tanzania', a study by the International Institute for Environment and Development (IIED), London 2009, available at pubs.iied.org.

3 Finnigan Wa Simbeye, 'This Dutch Firm is Cheating on Biofuel', *The Daily News*, 18 November, 2010, available at dailynews.co.tz.

4 Finnigan Wa Simbeye, 'Kisarawe Villagers Regret after Leasing Land to Sun Biofuels', *Tanzania Daily News*, 15 March 2010, available at allafrica.com.

5 Signed in 1997 in the Japanese city, the Kyoto Protocol for the reduction of global warming came into force in 2005. It envisaged the reduction in the period 2008–2012 of greenhouse gas emissions (carbon dioxide, methane, nitrogen oxide, hydrofluorocarbons, perfluorocarbons, and sulphur hexafluorides) by more than 5 percent of the amount in 1990. The United States signed the Protocol but subsequently refused to ratify it. China, India and other developing countries are exempt from the Protocol because they are not considered to be responsible for greenhouse gas emissions which, in the first industrialisation period, produced the present level of global warming.

6 On the link between agrofuel development projects and the possibility of obtaining carbon credits, as well as the impact of CDM on land grabbing in Africa, see 'The CDM and Africa: Marketing a New Land Grab', a briefing by the African Biodiversity Network, Biofuelwatch, Carbon Trade Watch, the Gaia Foundation and the Timberwatch Coalition, February 2011, available at oneplanetonly.org.

7 On this specific case see Blessing Karumbidza and Wally Menne, 'CDM Carbon Sink Trtee Plantations. A Case Study in Tanzania', 2010, a report by Timberwatch, a South African NGO Consortium, available at timberwatch.org.za.

Index

Index

Horn of Africa, 21, 23. *See also*
Ethiopia; Zenawi
House of Saud, royal family, 11,
69, 71, 75
houses, in Riyadh, 60–2
'humanitarian aid', 12, 21–2
Human Rights Council, 92–3
Human Rights Watch report, 19
'hunger riots' (2007-8), 121. *See
also* food crisis; investor(s) /
investment
hydroelectric energy (Ethiopia),
35–8
hydroponics technology, 74–6

IFAD (International Fund for
Agricultural Development),
83
IFC (International Finance
Corporation), 84, 101
IMF (International Monetary
Fund), 13, 83
INCRA (Instituto Nacional de
Colonização e Reforma
Agrária), 155–6
India
farmers' suicides in, 89
Karuturi acquisition group,
31–3, 38
Indonesia, 78, 82, 167
industrial farms. *See* agribusiness
companies
Indy Car Series, 129–32
inputs (fertilisers, pesticides,
seeds), 147–8
institutions (international),
contradictions of, 86–9. *See
also* IFC; neo-colonialism;
RAI; responsible investment;
UN; World Bank
Instituto Nacional de
Colonização e Reforma
Agrária (INCRA), 155–6
Interamerican Ethanol
Commission (Brazil/US),
158, 164
International Finance

Corporation (IFC), 84, 101
International Fund for
Agricultural Development
(IFAD), 83
'International Investment in
Agriculture' conference,
87–9
International Monetary Fund
(IMF), 13, 83
investor(s) / investment
absent from conferences, 93,
108
from commodities to land,
80–1, 100–1
De Schutter's conditions for,
92–3
versus farming tradition model,
88–9, 109–10, 193–4
financial instruments used,
80–1, 100–2, 126–7
and food crisis (2008), 90
for food security, 67, 69–70
in futures, 113–16, 120–1
on 'green revolution', 55, 89,
103, 110, 180–1
at Gulf Africa conference, 53–7
and hedging / speculation, 113,
127
labour costs to, 8–9, 97, 176,
188
and oral consent, 174–5
pension funds, 100–2, 126–7
and 'refuge goods', 121–3
retaining negotiated
government, 23–4
social responsibility, 98,
105–6, 108–10, 180
in water, 99–100
See also Chicago Mercantile
Exchange; food crisis; food
security; IFAD; IFC; IMF;
Lespinasse; RAI; responsible
investment; subsidies
Iowa Corn Growers Association,
129, 131
Iowa Renewable Fuels
Association, 129–30, 136

Index

Index

'five sisters' of, 146–8, 155
futures in (Ferruzzi
speculation), 115
and landed estates, 149–50
Soyatech, 93–4
'Special Rapporteur' de Schutter,
90–3, 110
speculators *(corner the market)*,
114–15. *See also* investor(s) /
investment
state investment, in rural
communities, 67, 69–70
Stedile, João Pedro (Movement of
Landless Workers), 161–7
Stookey, Hunt (HighQuest
Partners), 96–7
storage / distribution centers,
66–7, 112–13, 149. *See also*
food crisis; food security
subsidies
Saudi Arabia, 42–3, 44–5,
53–4
US, 128, 140, 159–60
Sudan, 45, 62–3, 67
sugarcane, 154–7, 165, 176. *See*
also agribusiness(es);
biofuels; Brazil; Mato Grosso
do Sul
suicide(s), 89, 145
Sun Biofuels, 35, 173–4, 176,
178
surveillance (Ethiopia), 26–7, 30.
See also EPRDF; Zenawi
swindle, by Bioshape (Tanzania),
176–7, 185
Syngenta (transnational), 148

Tanzania
biofuels investment in, 35,
175–6, 188–9
Biofuels Unit *Guidelines,*
183–6, 191–2
Bioshape swindle in, 176–7, 185
'carbon credit' investments in,
189–90
economic crisis, Mkindi on,
181

versus Ethiopia, 192–4
eucalyptus, in Mufindi region,
190
food for export in, 188–9
HakiArdhi research institute,
186
Investment Centre, 188
jatropha plantation in, 169–74
Kilwa project, 176, 185
Kisarawe district, 169–70,
172–4, 176, 182, 185
and labour costs, 188
Ministry of Energy and
Minerals, 182–3
Muhaga Village, 170–6, 182,
186, 193, 195–6
property laws in, 174–5
Simbeye on, 177
Sun Biofuels in, 35, 173–4,
176, 178
Yefred Myenzi interview in,
186–92, 194
taxi ride(s), in Riyadh, 51, 64–5
Thani, Hamad bin Khalifa Al, 57
'thermometer', traders as, 122–3,
126
Tigrinyas (Ethiopia), 18, 29. *See*
also EPRDF
traders (Chicago Mercantile
Exchange), 116–20
transnational companies. *See*
agribusiness(es)
Tropic and Cancer / Capricorn,
160–1, 175–6. *See also*
Rodrigues, Roberto

Uganda, 84
UN
CFS, 77–86, 90
FAO, 53, 77–80, 83, 136
Human Rights Council, 92–3
IFAD, 83
IFC, 84, 101
IMF, 13, 83
Special Rapporteur on the
Right to Food, 90–3, 110
See also World Bank